"This *Reader's Guide* is the most thorough literary study of *The Lion, the Witch and the Wardrobe* that I have ever read. It is a must for every serious student of Lewis's first Narnian Chronicle and a gateway to the entire series."

DR. PAUL F. FORD, AUTHOR OF *COMPANION TO NARNIA* AND *POCKET COMPANION TO NARNIA*

"A practical guide to an adult reading of C. S. Lewis's classic without losing the wonder of a child. It is informative, wise, inspiring and rich with insights into the kind of receptive reading that Lewis passionately encouraged. Not only does this *Reader's Guide* show the way into Narnia, but also into great literature, and the inexhaustible nourishment that great books provide."

COLIN DURIEZ, AUTHOR OF *A FIELD GUIDE TO NARNIA, THE C. S. LEWIS ENCYCLOPEDIA* AND *TOLKIEN AND C. S. LEWIS: THE GIFT OF FRIENDSHIP*

"*A Reader's Guide Through the Wardrobe* is that rare achievement, a literary guidebook that does not talk down to readers. It offers readable, informative help to adults who want to enjoy, understand and appreciate *The Lion, the Witch and the Wardrobe* fully as a literary work, not as a religious parable. Through detailed attention to structure, genres, techniques and themes, it shows how to read not just *LWW* but all works of fiction with sensitivity and insight."

PETER SCHAKEL, AUTHOR OF *APPROACHING LITERATURE IN THE 21ST CENTURY*

"This thorough, informative guide approaches C. S. Lewis's classic story the way Lewis himself read literary texts. It shows readers how to fully engage the narrative as thoughtful adults, while retaining a child's sense of wonder and delight."

DAVID C. DOWNING, AUTHOR OF *THE MOST RELUCTANT CONVERT, INTO THE REGION OF AWE* AND *INTO THE WARDROBE*

A
Reader's Guide
Through the Wardrobe

EXPLORING C. S. LEWIS'S
CLASSIC STORY

Leland Ryken
and Marjorie Lamp Mead

InterVarsity Press
Downers Grove, Illinois

InterVarsity Press
P.O. Box 1400, Downers Grove, IL 60515-1426
World Wide Web: www.ivpress.com
E-mail: mail@ivpress.com

InterVarsity Press® is the book-publishing division of InterVarsity Christian Fellowship/USA®, a student movement active on campus at hundreds of universities, colleges and schools of nursing in the United States of America, and a member movement of the International Fellowship of Evangelical Students. For information about local and regional activities, write Public Relations Dept., InterVarsity Christian Fellowship/USA, 6400 Schroeder Rd., P.O. Box 7895, Madison, WI 53707-7895, or visit the IVCF website at <www.intervarsity.org>.

See page 190 for further permission credit.

Design: Cindy Kiple

Images: wardrobe: Dominic Rouse/Getty Images
        winter forest scene: Paige Falk/istockphoto.com
        interior art: Used by permission of the Marion E Wade Center, Wheaton College, Wheaton, IL.

ISBN 0-8308-3289-0

Printed in the United States of America ∞

Library of Congress Cataloging-in-Publication Data

Ryken, Leland.
  A reader's guide through the wardrobe: exploring C. S. Lewis's
classic story / Leland Ryken and Marjorie Lamp Mead.
      p. cm.
  Includes bibliographical references and index.
  ISBN 0-8308-3289-0 (pbk.: alk. paper)
  1. Lewis, C. S. (Clive Staples), 1898-1963. Lion, the witch and the
wardrobe. 2. Children's stories, English—History and criticism. 3.
Christian fiction, English—History and criticism. 4. Fantasy
  I. Mead, Marjorie Lamp. II. Title.
  PR6023.E926L437 2005
  823'.912—dc22

                                                                    2005012002

P	19	18	17	16	15	14	13	12	11	10	9	8	7	6	5	4	3	2	1
Y	19	18	17	16	15	14	13	12	11	10	09	08	07		06		05			

To the memory of Emilie Rose Beaird

and

For Lyle and Mary Dorsett

Contents

PART 2: NARNIAN BACKGROUNDS

Introduction

For more than half a century C. S. Lewis's *The Lion, the Witch and the Wardrobe* has been a classic of children's literature. Indeed, in some circles it has been *the* classic children's story—the book in which many children discovered that they loved literature, the book that awakened their imagination and appetite for fantasy worlds. For many children it is also the book that awakened or enhanced their grasp of the Christian supernatural—the unseen transcendent reality that surrounds our everyday existence. One of the extraordinary things about Lewis's masterpiece is at what an early age children begin to relish the story (in our experience, as young as four is not uncommon).

But *The Lion, the Witch and the Wardrobe* is also paradoxically widely read by adults, who bring adult understanding and literary sophistication to it. Undoubtedly a majority of these adult readers were first introduced to the book in their own childhood. Many of them remain readers of the book because they, in turn, are reading the story to their own children and grandchildren. In this way, *The Lion, the Witch and the Wardrobe* has the status of a social institution by which succeeding generations of children are initiated into the pleasures of the book by adults who want them not to miss a good thing. Such adult readers actually experience the story on two levels—the level of the children to whom they read the book and also their own level as mature readers who have a superior grasp of the nuances of the story. The ability of the book to hold its readers into their late years is perhaps just as remarkable as how early it attracts the young.

We have written a reader's guide for adult readers of *The Lion, the Witch and the Wardrobe*. As a new movie version of the story is released, likely even more adults will find themselves interested in revisiting a classic tale from their childhood, while some who have never read this story will be attracted to it for the first time. For all readers who wish to reflect on the book or discuss it with others from an adult vantage point, our reader's guide is an ideal companion.

THE NATURE OF THIS BOOK

This reader's guide to *The Lion, the Witch and the Wardrobe* is based on four guiding principles:

- If you haven't already read *The Lion, the Witch and the Wardrobe* in its entirety at least once, please do so *before* you go on to chapter two. This guide is intended to accompany you on *subsequent* readings of the book, not to flavor your initial, very personal experience of the story. We cannot emphasize this enough. Your own enjoyment will be greatly enhanced if upon your first reading you simply allow this wonderful story to unfold before you. Lewis himself would recommend this approach.

- But once you have truly experienced *The Lion, the Witch and the Wardrobe* in its fullness as a story, then please turn back once more to this volume. We have gathered a variety of useful material that will enrich your understanding of this splendid tale and thereby ultimately deepen your enjoyment of it.

- Our primary approach to *The Lion, the Witch and the Wardrobe* is to look at it through lenses gathered from Lewis's literary criticism on the subject of literature and literary analysis. The result can be described as "reading *The Lion, the Witch and the Wardrobe* with C. S. Lewis."

- The commentary we provide on *The Lion, the Witch and the Wardrobe* in chapter two is envisioned as a guide to solitary reflection or discussion in a group setting. We have accordingly interspersed prompts to reflection and discussion throughout the guide. Even this is something that Lewis espoused. In one of his books of literary criticism, he wrote, "Oddly as it may sound, I conceive that it is the chief duty of the interpreter to begin analyses and to leave them unfinished," thereby serving a function to "awaken" and "stir" responses and perceptions from a literary critic's reader.

For ease of reading, our chapters in part 1 correspond with Lewis's chapters in *The Lion, the Witch and the Wardrobe* and even bear the same main titles.

UNLESS YOU BECOME AS A CHILD: READING FOR ENJOYMENT FIRST

Who is the better reader of *The Lion, the Witch and the Wardrobe*—the child or the adult? The answer is not as easy as one might think. There are some significant ways in which the child's response is better and should remain the model toward which adult readers aspire.

Lewis himself said something close to this in his commentary on Edmund Spenser's long narrative poem *The Faerie Queene*. Lewis was of the opinion that this epic poem demanded to be read on two levels: there is obvious benefit from employing a sophisticated literary approach, but just as important is a simple and childlike receptivity. As Lewis explained, "Its primary appeal is to the most naïve and innocent tastes. . . . It demands of us a child's love of marvels and dread of bogies, a boy's thirst for adventures. . . . The poem is a great palace, but the door into it is so low that you must stoop to go in. . . . It is of course much more than a fairy-tale, but unless we can enjoy it as a fairy-tale *first of all*, we shall not really care for it." These perceptive observations on how to approach Spenser's epic are equally applicable to other examples of fantasy literature, including Lewis's own children's stories. We read such stories best when we read with the heart of a child.

Accordingly, to read *The Lion, the Witch and the Wardrobe* in the spirit with which Lewis wrote and read fairy stories, we need to read for enjoyment first. Children experience a story at the level of sheer enjoyment, unencumbered by inquiry into allegorical meanings and theological implications. Too often readers assume that Lewis began writing his children's stories with an intentional Christian objective and *then* crafted a story to express his meaning. This was decidedly not the case. As Lewis recounted, when he wrote the Narnian stories "everything began with images; a faun carrying an umbrella, a queen on a sledge, a magnificent lion. At first there wasn't even anything Christian about them; that element pushed itself in of its own accord." In other words, the imaginative impulse definitely came first in Lewis's creative process.

Why is a proper understanding of this relationship between the imagination and moral purpose so significant? Because adult readers who mistakenly believe that Lewis's primary intention in writing his fiction was to convey religious ideas will tend to leapfrog over the story in order to search for the "hidden" message. In so doing, they not only risk distorting the theological meaning but also may miss the wonder of the story itself.

The theological imagination operates by the rules of the imagination, not by the rules of the rational intellect. It produces stories and poems, not essays. Before we can understand a work produced by the theological imagination, we must take time to enjoy the story or poem. As Lewis's friend and former pupil George Sayer explained, "[Lewis] wanted the moral and spiritual significance of his works of fiction to be assimilated subliminally, if at all, and he was annoyed when his publisher outlined the theme of *Out of the Silent Planet* [one of his science fiction novels] in the blurb on the dust jacket. Over and over again in talking about his fiction, he would say, 'But it's there for the story.'"

Thus our first and essential step in the reading process must simply be to enjoy. This approach has its own rewards, for if we allow ourselves to wholeheartedly enter the story with our imaginations—to look, listen, surrender and receive, as Lewis advised—then "we shall be deliciously surprised by the satisfaction of wants we were not aware of till they were satisfied."

PAST WATCHFUL DRAGONS: THE INDIRECTNESS OF THE THEOLOGICAL IMAGINATION

The theological imagination achieves its theological purposes by means of what we can call *delayed action insight.* We begin by enjoying the narrative and entering its imagined world. Engaged in this way, the story seemingly has no theological designs on us. But gradually it dawns on us that more has been embodied and communicated than simply a narrative. Thus even though immersion in the story is the first item on a reader's agenda, this does not preclude a further and equally significant purpose of the story: to awaken us to theological truths, helping us to observe, understand and experience spiritual realities in a deeper and more meaningful way than we otherwise would.

Speaking specifically of his Narnian stories, C. S. Lewis described his strategy this way:

> I thought I saw how stories of this kind could steal past a certain inhibition which had paralysed much of my own religion in childhood. Why did one find it so hard to feel as one was told one ought to feel about God or about the sufferings of Christ? I thought the chief reason was that one was told one ought to. An obligation to feel can freeze feelings. . . . But supposing that by casting all these things into an imaginary world, stripping them of their stained-glass and Sunday School associations, one could make them for the first time appear in their real potency? Could one not thus steal past these watchful dragons? I thought one could.

Elsewhere Lewis affirms that aid in overcoming their own emotional barriers to faith was something he saw as necessary for both his young and adult readers. In other words, Lewis was not simply packaging theology in the form of fantasy in order to reach those too young to read works of apologetics. Instead he recognized the power of fantasy to reach all ages, regardless of educational background or intellectual ability. The success of Lewis's strategy is eloquently illustrated in the following account by award-winning author Katherine Paterson, as she recalls the effect of Lewis's Narnian tales in her own life:

Over twenty years ago a college English professor said something that has bothered me ever since. He wondered aloud if it was possible to describe Christian experience effectively except by fantasy or science fiction. I've tried to fight this view, because I don't write fantasy or science fiction. But he may be right. I say this as one haunted by visions of the great lion Aslan, whose bright goodness never fails to flood my spirit with awe and joy. I was once very much involved with a young man who, when I tried to share with him my love for C. S. Lewis's Chronicles of Narnia, said earnestly that he felt it was wrong of Lewis to distort the Bible in this way. I should have known at that moment that the relationship was doomed. Aslan is not a distortion but a powerful symbol of the Lion of Judah, which can nourish our spirits as the reasoned arguments of a thousand books of theology can never do. We can dare to face the dark, because we've had a shining glimpse of the light.

This is what a story like *The Lion, the Witch and the Wardrobe* does best: it awakens us to the transcendent light shining all around—the bright gleam of divine reality that we could not apprehend as effectively through our reason alone.

A BOOK FOR ALL SEASONS

While this guide is addressed to adult readers who want to read *The Lion, the Witch and the Wardrobe* at a sophisticated literary level, we have suggested that the ideal reader is also attuned to *the child within*. At its core, *The Lion, the Witch and the Wardrobe* is a book about children, written for children. This reader's guide keeps this foundation constantly in view. But as Lewis himself said, "A children's story which is enjoyed only by children is a bad children's story. The good ones last." Lewis also declared that he enjoyed fairy tales better as an adult than he did in his childhood.

The Lion, the Witch and the Wardrobe is ready to meet you at whatever level you are prepared to receive it. At the simplest level, we can read it for its plot—to find out what happens next and how it turns out. At a more advanced level, we can read for the pleasures of characterization and of entering the imagined world of the story, with the realization that worldmaking is one of Lewis' most characteristic gifts as a storyteller. If we have read widely enough, we will naturally be receptive to the archetypal patterns in the book, as well as the impressive range of literary genres that converge in it. At a more specialized level of response, we can relish the "how" of the story—the exquisite style and techniques that doubtless account for the staying power of all the Narnian stories.

Lewis was a champion of the idea that the less sophisticated levels of reading—reading like very young children, in a sense—are not bad, they are simply incomplete. After listing the ways in which the unliterary read stories, Lewis writes, "Let us be quite clear that the unliterary are unliterary not because they enjoy stories in these ways, but because they enjoy them in no other. . . . For *all these enjoyments* are shared by good readers reading good books." We hope, then, that this reader's guide will help you to continue to enjoy *The Lion, the Witch and the Wardrobe* in all the ways you have read it in the past, as well as encourage you to learn new perspectives and approaches that may enhance your future enjoyment and understanding of this and other stories. As Lewis wrote to his boyhood friend and literary companion Arthur Greeves, "Re-reading old favourites is . . . one of my greatest pleasures: indeed, I can't imagine a man really enjoying a book and reading it only once."

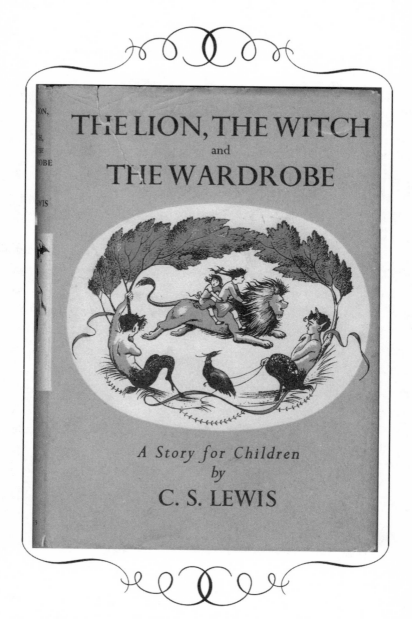

First edition cover of *The Lion, the Witch and the Wardrobe* (1950), Geoffrey Bles publisher.

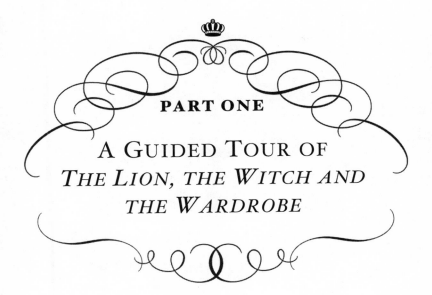

PART ONE

A GUIDED TOUR OF *THE LION, THE WITCH AND THE WARDROBE*

I

Lucy Looks into a Wardrobe
How the Story Begins

Great stories have many key moments, but the two greatest tests of a storyteller are beginning the story well and ending it well. The first of these two is the most important of all, for the simple reason that if a book's opening does not captivate a reader, the battle has been lost. The author of *First Paragraphs: Inspired Openings for Writers and Readers*, calls a book's opening paragraph "the first welling of life that gives breath to a piece of writing."

"*Every novelist . . . has known the exciting but intimidating challenge of that first sentence. . . . Everyone has had to begin somewhere.*"

GEORGIANNE ENSIGN, *GREAT BEGINNINGS*

The means by which storytellers successfully seize their readers' attention vary widely. Once alerted to them, we can begin to see which of them are present in the opening paragraphs of *The Lion, the Witch and the Wardrobe*. Here is a sampling of some famous openings:

- "This is the story of a man who was never at a loss" (Homer, *The Odyssey*).
- "Once upon a time" (universal—part of the racial or collective unconscious).
- "Call me Ishmael" (Herman Melville, *Moby Dick*).
- "Once when Jacob was cooking stew, Esau came in from the field, and he was exhausted" (the biblical story of Jacob and Esau, Genesis 25:29).
- "As Gregor Samsa awoke one morning from uneasy dreams he found himself

transformed in his bed into a gigantic insect" (Franz Kafka, *Metamorphosis*).

- "Five friends I had, and two of them snakes" (Frederick Buechner, *Godric*).
- "The towers of zenith aspired above the morning mist; austere towers of steel and cement and limestone, sturdy as cliffs and delicate as silver rods. They were neither citadels nor churches, but frankly and beautifully office-buildings" (Sinclair Lewis, *Babbitt*).

There is obviously no scarcity of ways by which storytellers can manage the feat of "hooking" a reader at the outset of a story. They may introduce something unusual and out of the normal routine. Conversely, many stories put before us something totally realistic and commonplace. Some storytellers bewitch us with a touch of fantasy or suspense. Others plunge us immediately into a compelling action. Storytellers can win us with vivid description or humor. Sometimes the very style is so sparkling that our appetite for the story is immediately aroused.

The Story Begins: First Lines in the Chronicles of Narnia

- *"Once there were four children whose names were Peter, Susan, Edmund and Lucy, and it has been told in another book called* The Lion, the Witch and the Wardrobe *how they had a remarkable adventure"* (Prince Caspian, 1950).
- *"There was a boy called Eustace Clarence Scrubb, and he almost deserved it"* (The Voyage of the "Dawn Treader," 1952).
- *"It was a dull autumn day and Jill Pole was crying behind the gym"* (The Silver Chair, 1953).
- *"This is the story of an adventure that happened in Narnia and Calormen and the lands between, in the Golden Age when Peter was High King in Narnia and his brother and his two sisters were King and Queens under him"* (The Horse and His Boy, 1954).
- *"This is a story about something that happened long ago when your grandfather was a child"* (The Magician's Nephew, 1955).
- *"In the last days of Narnia, far up to the west beyond Lantern Waste and close beside the great waterfall, there lived an Ape"* (The Last Battle, 1956).

Regardless of what techniques a writer uses, the key business that must be transacted is the element of *transport*. The opening of a story must transport us from the time and place we are literally occupying to an imagined time and place. Such transport is an escape in the good sense of the term, and no one has written better on it than C. S. Lewis: "There is a clear sense in which all reading whatever is an escape. It involves a temporary transference of the mind from our actual surroundings to things merely imagined or conceived. . . . All such escape is *from* the same thing; immediate, concrete actuality."

For simple narrative forms like fairy tales and children's stories, a time-honored formula has been "Once upon a time." Tom Howard observed that "once upon a time in a far off land" is "the best opening for a story—there's no question about it. For at that point we can settle in. There's no danger of any clutter and intrusion from the immediate world."

For Reflection or Discussion

- For you personally, what are the techniques and effects by which Lewis interests you in the story that he is beginning in *The Lion, the Witch and the Wardrobe*?
- As you ponder that question, you might profitably bring to bear your knowledge that stories consist of three main ingredients—plot or action, characters and settings—and that any one of these might pique your interest in the opening moments of a story.
- Lewis begins his fantasy story with utterly commonplace realism, describing children in an actual historical moment (England during World War II) and a true-to-life British house in the country. What are the effects of Lewis's beginning with realism? At what point do you begin to suspect that this world will open up into a fantasy world?

C. S. Lewis and Children

Lewis's friend Roger Lancelyn Green makes it clear that while the Narnian stories were being written, they "were not told to actual children; nor had [Lewis] any but the most superficial acquaintance with the species at the time of writing." In fact, autumn 1939 and thereafter, when evacuee children stayed in Lewis's home during the war, was one of the few periods when Lewis was living in close proximity to children on a daily basis (the other occurred when he married Joy Davidman in 1956 and became stepfather to her two sons). He displayed a natural reserve with children, writing to his friend Arthur Greeves, "I theoretically hold that one ought to like children, but am shy with them in practice." Yet Lewis took the time to write many kind and informative letters to his young fans, including one where he responded: "No, I didn't start with four real children in mind: I just made them up."

THE INITIATION MOTIF

The opening paragraphs transact the necessary business of getting the story started. The remainder of the first chapter is an initiation story, in a double sense. We as readers are initiated into the narrative world of the book, while within the story itself, the children are initiated into the world that we enter with them. Two things occupy us in the beginning—assembling the cast of characters and describing the country house that the children set out to explore.

The opening sentence tells us that "once there were four children whose names were Peter, Susan, Edmund and Lucy." Naming is of course important to all stories, but perhaps preeminently so for children's stories. Four more characters are named on the first page. The Professor is also introduced, but surprisingly, he is not named, being instead referred to by his professional title.

Since this is a children's fantasy story with affinities to the folk-literature genre of the beast fable (a story with animal characters), we could almost predict that animals will join the cast of characters. They do—not yet in the full-fledged fantasy version of the talking animals of Narnia, but rather in the domesticated version of country animals that the children imagine might inhabit the countryside where they now reside.

ℭℯ *For Reflection or Discussion*

- First impressions count for a lot in stories, partly because they set up expectations that are both fulfilled and revised as the story unfolds. What are your earliest impressions of the characters?

- Whatever stands out from the common ground is often important in stories. Eight characters are named on the first page of this story, but the Professor is not named, being known to us only by a professional title. What is the effect of this omission of the professor's name?

- The animals that the children imagine as being natives of the region evoke the pastoral tradition that idealizes the countryside in contrast to the city (here represented by London during wartime). In addition to priming the reader for the pastoral dimension of Narnia, what is the significance of this book's beginning on an idyllic pastoral note?

THE PROFESSOR'S HOUSE: A TOUCH OF THE GOTHIC

It would be an overstatement to say that the rambling, nearly empty country house that greets us at the start of *The Lion, the Witch and the Wardrobe* is a haunted house. It obviously has its attractive features, and it is child-friendly as well as a tourist attraction. But the house of the opening chapter does not rank as a cozy home. It is "a far larger house than [Lucy] had ever been in before," with many "long passages and rows of doors leading into empty rooms," and its sheer size begins to make Lucy feel "a little creepy" (*LWW*, ch. 1, p. 5).*

---

*The edition of *The Lion, the Witch and the Wardrobe* used in this guide is the 1994 hardcover HarperCollins edition, with color illustrations by Chris Van Allsburg.

If you consult a handbook of literary terms, you will find the following descriptors for the literary form known as "the gothic": evocation of primitive feelings of horror; presence of the mysterious and supernatural; forlorn settings such as dreary landscapes, graveyards, deserted castles or dungeons, or big old houses with lots of empty rooms; rainy or stormy weather to enhance a mood of gloom or foreboding. Ghost scenes are a favorite device.

For Reflection or Discussion

The Professor's house is ambivalent—both good and scary. It is the main feature of the middle of chapter 1 and was obviously important to the author's design. Look carefully in the text for clues as to its meaning, and in the process allow the house to come alive in your imagination. You might also recall similar houses in your literary memory or in real-life experience.

THE STRANGE WORLD MOTIF

The last piece of narrative business in chapter 1 is to move Lucy into Narnia for the first time. Of course as readers we enter Narnia with Lucy. The magic of the experience never ends: the backless wardrobe, the snow crunching underfoot, the cold woods, the lamp-post, the pitter-patter of the Faun's feet, the Faun himself with his gift parcels.

The literary motif at work in our first entry into Narnia is known as "the journey to a strange world." This genre places a premium on the creative activity that through the centuries has usually been called inventiveness—the ability not simply to make up fictional details but, beyond that, to imagine places, characters and events that do not exist in the world of waking reality. In a work of literary theory that C. S. Lewis admired, sixteenth-century English writer Sir Philip Sidney praised creative

Little Lea

When C. S. Lewis was seven, his family moved into a new home in a prosperous East Belfast neighborhood. This large, rambling home contained many rooms where young "Jack" (C. S.) and his brother Warnie could happily play, but it was

the attic spaces that gave them the most enjoyment. Here they had a private room of their very own, where they could paint and write without needing to worry about tidying up. The Little End Room, as they called it, also offered wonderful views of the surrounding countryside—scenery of exquisite and elusive beauty which fed the imaginative heart of the young Lewis. "I am a product of long corridors, empty sunlit rooms, upstair indoor silences, attics explored in solitude, distant noises of gurgling cisterns and pipes, and the noise of wind under the tiles." This photograph was taken by Warren Lewis in 1919 when he was home on leave from World War I Belgium.

writers for their ability to imagine things that are nonexistent in our world. A creative writer, said Sidney, "disdaining to be tied to [imitation of the known world], lifted up with the vigour of his own invention, doth grow in effect another nature, in making things either better than Nature bringeth forth, or, quite anew, forms such as never were in Nature." Lewis interpreted this as a claim "to limitless freedom of invention," a prerogative that he himself exercised when creating Narnia. We should note in passing that in the twentieth century, J. R. R. Tolkien reformulated Sidney's theory of the writer as creator of another world in his theory of the writer as subcreator.

Lewis Family Wardrobe

This dark oak wardrobe, which is more than one hundred years old, was hand carved by Lewis's grandfather and originally stood in the family home of Little Lea in Belfast. Later it was moved to the Kilns, Lewis's home outside Oxford. In 1973, it was purchased by the Marion E. Wade Center and brought to Wheaton College, Illinois. Years later, one of Lewis's cousins, Claire Lewis Clapperton, described occasions when various cousins, along with C. S. Lewis ("Jack") and his brother Warren, would climb into the wardrobe and listen quietly "while Jack told us his tales of adventure."

It is not difficult to see how the childhood storytelling sessions that took place within the wardrobe later evolved in Lewis's mind into the idea of using a wardrobe as the doorway into Narnia. You can also hear echoes of the young boy sitting in the dark and telling his "tales of adventure," all the while keeping in view a crack of light where the wardrobe door was ajar, in the adult author's reminder to his readers that Lucy had left the door open "of course, because she knew that it is foolish to shut oneself into any wardrobe" (LWW, ch. 1, p. 7).

Just how effectively Lewis communicates to his readers in this scene can be observed in the reaction of the children (and many adults!) who come to see the Lewis family wardrobe in the museum of the Marion E. Wade Center. Energetic children who would never give a similar piece of furniture a second glance pause before this lovely antique and reach out to gently touch the carved swirls on its dark oak doors. They ask questions: "Is this the wardrobe?" "Can I look inside?" "Why does it have a back?" They consider it thoughtfully, often with a quiet little smile. They know this great wooden object towering over them is somehow special—after all, they have read the story!

Of course C. S. Lewis did not make up all his otherworldly details "from scratch." Many other inventive writers through the centuries had created a storehouse of imaginary creatures. An example is the Faun who is sprung on us at the end of chapter 1. Like many other of the mythical and fantastic creatures in this book, the Faun came by way of the mythological past. From classical times onward, fauns had these traits: they were forest dwellers; their

---

"The Lion all began with a picture of a Faun carrying an umbrella and parcels in a snowy wood. This picture had been in my mind since I was about sixteen. Then one day, when I was about forty, I said to myself: 'Let's try to make a story about it.'"

C. S. LEWIS, "IT ALL BEGAN WITH A PICTURE"

---

lower torso was that of a goat; their upper torso was at least partly human, though they were often pictured as having goat's horns and pointed ears. In their classical origins, fauns were animalistic and debauched, but in the transmutations that occurred through the centuries, they were sometimes pictured as being gentle, rustic and essentially human. Such were the endearing fauns of which Lewis was so fond in Edmund Spenser's *Faerie Queene*—figures of natural innocence and virtue who add "jocundity and jollity" to the story.

For Reflection or Discussion

Several fruitful avenues exist to aid us in assimilating our entry into Narnia in the last third of chapter 1.

- The impressionistic question: what are your own favorite details in this initial journey into Narnia in *The Lion, the Witch and the Wardrobe*?
- List the elements of foreshadowing (especially if you are familiar with the rest of the story) embodied in some of the specific details Lewis plants in this preliminary sketch of Narnia.

- We need to make sense of the nature of the Faun, who is obviously a triumph of Lewis's mythic imagination. What specifically do you picture? Why did Lewis choose to include the particular details about Mr. Tumnus that we find in the initial description of him?

FINAL IMPRESSIONS

To be a thoughtful reader, you need to pause at the end of every chapter in a story and take stock of what has transpired, what has been established in the chapter and what your final impressions are. To aid the process of reflection on the opening chapter of *The Lion, the Witch and the Wardrobe*, recall the main sequence: arrival of the children at a country house during wartime; brief introductory glimpses of the four siblings and their relationships; the strange new world of the big, rambling house that the children decide to explore on a rainy day, followed by the even stranger world of Narnia into which Lucy stumbles. What stands out most vividly? What details seem to you most laden with potential significance at this early stage of the story? What details speak most powerfully to your imagination? Above all, codify—that is, list and arrange—your understanding of what you have been *initiated into* in chapter 1.

The Lamp-post

One of the details that Lewis includes in the first chapter is the surprising placement of a lamp-post in the middle of a snowy woods. There are those who believe that Lewis's imagination was sparked by the Victorian-era gas lamp-posts he had observed when he was a young boy living as a boarding student in Malvern, England. Years later, Lewis told his friend George Sayer (who lived and taught in Malvern) how much he had enjoyed the soft glow of these gas lamps on the hillsides. This particular lamp-post is located in front of the Malvern Priory, where Lewis attended worship services during his visits to the Sayer's home.

2

What Lucy Found There
Discovering More About the Strange World

The opening chapter included an entry from the known world into the strange world of Narnia. But we did not learn anything about the world that Lucy and we have entered, other than that it is a snowy woods. Chapter 2 has as its purpose to give us a fuller understanding of Narnia. At this early point in the story, we are like detectives arriving on a crime scene and starting to gather data (actually, at the beginning of the story Narnia *is* a crime scene—a world being tyrannized by a wicked witch).

The main sequence in chapter 2 is this: Lucy and the Faun make acquaintance and exchange preliminary information about their respective situations; the two travel deeper into the forest and enter a cave that turns out to be Mr. Tumnus's home; Lucy has a look around and enjoys a really luscious tea; bad news emerges as Mr. Tumnus clues Lucy (and us) in to the evil grip that the White Witch exercises over Narnia, and further that Mr. Tumnus has orders to betray to the White Witch the presence of any human who arrives in Narnia; Mr. Tumnus is overcome with grief at the thought of betraying Lucy, so the two quietly steal back to the wardrobe door, whereupon Lucy reenters the big house that the four siblings are in the process of exploring.

UTOPIAN CONVENTIONS

The literary genre at work in chapter 2 is the utopian journey to a strange world, but not exactly in the sense the word *utopia* has for most people today. *Utopia* is based on a Greek phrase meaning "no place"; that is its primary meaning. It is also a pun on a Greek word meaning "good place." It is the first meaning that is important early in the story, though the second meaning enters in the later stages of the story.

Sixteenth-century English writer Thomas More coined the word *utopia* and wrote the first self-conscious utopia in Western literature. The key elements in the genre include these:

- creation of an alternate world, not simply a replica of the known world
- imagining a geography for the strange world
- populating the strange world with creatures that are partly different from those in the world around us

In a discussion of Thomas More's *Utopia,* C. S. Lewis himself gives us some of the best commentary on the utopian genre. While acknowledging that More's fictional world has "a thread of serious thought running through it," the element that Lewis stresses is the way in which More "gives his imagination free rein." To succeed with an imaginary "other" world, an author needs to relish the fun of imagining that world. When we read that the land of Narnia encompasses "all that lies between the lamp-post and the great castle of Cair Paravel on the eastern sea" (*LWW,* ch. 2, p. 12), we should thrill to the authentic utopian note of "nowhere"; in other words, we find ourselves in a place outside the boundaries of our known world.

Because Lewis was a devotee of the mythical imagination, the "nowhere" quality in his fiction is always capable of turning in a mythical direction. We get an early instance during the teatime conversation in which Mr. Tumnus tells Lucy tales involving the Nymphs, the Dryads, the Fauns, the Red Dwarfs, and even Silenus and "Bacchus himself." The mythical dimension of Narnia is obviously important to Lewis; we keep learning more and more about this as we progress through *The Lion, the Witch and the Wardrobe.*

An additional analytic grid that we need to have constantly in mind as we read a fictional account of an alternate world is the way that world relates to

The Imaginary World of Boxen

"[Thomas More] *says many things for the fun of them, surrendering himself to the sheer pleasure of imagined geography, imagined language, and imagined institutions. That is what readers whose interests are rigidly political do not understand: but everyone who has ever made an imaginary map responds at once."* When Lewis makes a comment such as this, he is reflecting back to his own childhood and the maps he made of his own imaginary world, Boxen. Created together with his brother, this imaginary world combined Warnie's passion for steamships and trains with Jack's interest in "dressed animals" (in the tradition of Beatrix Potter) and chivalric knights. The notebooks containing these childhood drawings and stories were carefully preserved by the brothers and eventually willed by Warren Lewis to the Marion E. Wade Center at Wheaton College, where they are available for use by researchers.

our own world. When William Shakespeare, for example, in *A Midsummer Night's Dream*, creates a magical forest to which residents of Athens find their way, he intends that we view the forest, for all its far-flung fantasy, as a mirror of our world. The fantastic world simply rearranges the form in which the issues of the real world appear. In the case of Shakespeare's play, the difficulties of the young in winning their true loves is carried right over from Athens to the magical woods. In stories that juxtapose our own world and a strange world, we swing back and forth between the familiar and the unfamiliar. One moment we are simply relishing the adventure of what we find in the strange world, and the next we are reminded of the problems of our own world and our lives in it.

✎ *For Reflection or Discussion*

Before moving through the chapter in sequence, it is important to have the foregoing utopian framework in place as a lens through which to observe what happens in chapter 2. Here are some specific things to look for:

- What imaginary, unlifelike details and qualities of Narnia capture your imagination and strike you as simply entertaining?
- What recognizable human experience comes through the strange details and creatures of Narnia?
- What deeper problems of the real world, especially regarding the threatening nature of evil, unsettle you and subvert an otherwise delightful excursion into Narnia?

SURFACE PLEASANTRIES: HUMOR AND BRITISHNESS

There is much that is lighthearted as we follow Lucy and Mr. Tumnus to his house. Some of it is humorous, as in Mr. Tumnus's mistaking "spare room" as "Spare Oom" and "wardrobe" as "War Drobe" (*LWW*, ch. 2, p. 13). The cozy cave with two little chairs ("one for me and one for a friend" [*LWW*, ch. 2, p. 14]) surely evokes a smile, as do the details of what Lucy and Mr. Tumnus eat. The book titles on the shelf in the cave contain a subtle humor, as in *Is Man a Myth?* At such moments we can say about Lewis what he said about More's *Utopia*: "he does not keep our noses to the grindstone. He says many things for the fun of them."

Another source of pleasantry for non-British readers (and perhaps for British readers as well) is the British flavor of *The Lion, the Witch and the Wardrobe*. In attempting to account for the popularity of C. S. Lewis among American evangelicals, Philip Graham Ryken lists as one of five reasons his "Britishness." This is present from the very beginning of the book: on the first page there is a reference to children being sent to the country during air raids on London. It is also there on the next two pages, with the idiomatic "old chap" and the reference to "a wireless." Even the "wonderful tea" that Lucy enjoys at the hospitality of Mr. Tumnus is a set piece of Britishness.

For Reflection or Discussion

At any point in *The Lion, the Witch and the Wardrobe* the latent humor of some of the details, as well as the pervasive Britishness of the expressions, settings and events, is something to relish. If these aspects of the story really interest you, you can evolve an anatomy of types of humor and categories of British qualities. You may also want to reflect on how differently you might feel about the story if it had been set in modern-day New York City. What would be lost if the Britishness were removed from the story?

HOW DOES NARNIA RELATE TO OUR OWN WORLD?

The issue of the relationship between Narnia and our own world will become increasingly important as the book unfolds, but it is introduced in chapter 2 in a way that requires us to keep our antennae up regarding the issue. Mr. Tumnus's early question whether Lucy is "a Daughter of Eve," (*LWW,* ch. 2, p. 11) soon followed by the question whether she is "in fact Human," already teases us into wondering what is at stake. Near the end of the chapter, we learn that the White Witch has ordered her spies to inform her if they ever see "a Son of Adam or a Daughter of Eve in the wood" (*LWW,* ch. 2, p. 20). Even the capitalizing of the words in these epithets hints at something significant, though we do not at this early point know what that significance is.

What we have here is a microcosm of what is happening throughout chapter 2. We are being given preliminary glimpses only of what Narnia is like. Some of the details are in a code language that we still need to decipher. Part of the rhythm of narrative is that we intuitively begin to make guesses, some of which are validated and others disproved as the story unfolds.

For Reflection or Discussion

If you want to get maximum mileage out of chapter 2, you can make a list of the details that you suspect are foreshadowings of important developments later to come.

PREMONITIONS OF EVIL

The Lion, the Witch and the Wardrobe is a story of danger and threat. Chapter 2 exists to establish the dire nature of the threat without delineating the details. An early signpost is Mr. Tumnus's observation that "it is winter in Narnia, and has been for ever so long" (*LWW*, p. 12). Mr. Tumnus's crying fit, followed by the news that he is in service to the White Witch and under orders to kidnap any humans who stumble into Narnia, greatly intensifies our fears. In fact, halfway through, chapter 2 becomes an ever-expanding list of ominous details about the extent of the power of evil in Narnia.

> ### ℘ *For Reflection or Discussion*
> Collect the evidences of evil and threat, and consider the effect of the chapter ending's enclosure of these early hints of evil in a reassuring framework with the charming picture of Lucy's running back to the wardrobe "as quickly as her legs would carry her" (*LWW*, ch. 2, p. 22), momentarily leaving the vision of evil behind.

3
Edmund and the Wardrobe
Characterization

Stories are a delicate balancing act among three main ingredients: setting, plot and character. The perennial temptation among readers and critics is to elevate one of these and slight the others. To do so impoverishes our experience of any well-told story (though it is also possible for storytellers themselves to disrupt the balance that should exist). We have somewhat arbitrarily chosen to introduce the concept of characterization in *The Lion, the Witch and the Wardrobe* with our analysis of the third chapter, but keep in mind that what we say about characterization here applies to every chapter in the book.

The importance of characterization in *The Lion, the Witch and the Wardrobe* was highlighted for one of us recently when not-quite-four Bethany and just-turned-four Jacob were "talking shop" about *The Lion, the Witch and the Wardrobe* in the back seat of the car.

"Who is your favorite character?" queried Bethany.

"Lucy," replied Jacob.

The exchange was rooted in sound narrative theory. It was first of all a tribute to the importance of characters in the story. The question about a *favorite* character correctly implied, moreover, that characterization achieves its ends by *affective* means (getting us to feel certain ways about the characters) and further that a story ordinarily has an engaging central character who is the protagonist and hero.

When we praise some storytellers for remarkable powers of characterization (Geoffrey Chaucer, William Shakespeare and Charles Dickens spring immediately to mind), we usually have in mind the following specific skills:

- the ability to create universal character types, so that we feel as though we have known the characters in real life
- balancing that, the ability to create unique characters whom we know only in the stories in which they appear
- vividness in description of characters, including their visual appearance
- ability to create characters who elicit strong reader response, either positive (heroic characters whom we admire) or negative (villains who awaken our fear and contempt)
- creation of characters whose experiences are identical to ours, so that we identify strongly with them

What is most essential for storytellers is that they lead readers to care about what happens to the characters in their stories. One literary critic,

Sheldon Sacks, uses the helpful formula "characters about whose fates we are made to care."

> ## ○ *For Reflection or Discussion*
> Most readers would rank C. S. Lewis as good at characterization. Using the foregoing list of skills as a point of reference, what things constitute Lewis's skill with characterization for you personally? Which characters do you find yourself especially identifying with? Whose destiny have you begun to care about?

CHARACTERS AS EMBODIMENTS OF MEANING

Ultimately every aspect of a story helps to embody the meanings of the story, for literary form (the "how" of an utterance) determines the meaning; the medium is the message. In a story, there is no meaning apart from the settings, characters and action. It is not uncommon for characters to embody a particularly important share of the meaning. Put another way, a lot of what storytellers want to say about life is embodied in the characters they create.

"In most good stories it is the character's personality
that creates the action of the story. . . . If you start with a real personality,
a real character, then something is bound to happen;
and you don't have to know what before you begin.
In fact it may be better if you don't know what before you begin.
You ought to be able to discover something from your stories."

FLANNERY O'CONNOR, *MYSTERY AND MANNERS*

The starting point for seeing how this is true is to understand that characters in a story are representative of people generally. Writers project our own human experiences onto characters. Flannery O'Connor thus claimed that "any character in a serious novel is supposed to carry a burden of meaning larger than himself." Lewis was of a similar opinion about the way literary characters embody universal human experience. He takes up the subject in a famous essay on Shakespeare's character Hamlet, and his claim is that we are interested in Hamlet because his speeches "describe so well a certain spiritual region through which most of us have passed."

With this framework before us as a lens, we can turn to the unfolding action of chapter 3 of *The Lion, the Witch and the Wardrobe*, casting retrospective glances at chapters 1-2 whenever it's appropriate.

LUCY AND EDMUND AS FOILS

The opening pages of chapter 3 bring out into the open certain aspects of the four siblings that have been established faintly in the preceding two chapters. One of these is the unpleasantness of Edmund as a person. (You might wish to backtrack and see how the seeds of Edmund's negative character traits are planted in chapters 1-2.)

Another feature that receives progressive treatment at the start of chapter 3 is the characterization of Lucy as the central figure of the story—the protagonist and heroine (the word *protagonist* is based on the Greek words meaning "first struggler"—the one from whose viewpoint we go through the action). The specific literary role that Lucy fills in the episode in which her siblings mistrust her account of having been to Narnia is famous in the world's literature. It is called *the spurned female* (someone has written a whole book on the spurned woman in Shakespeare).

Characterization is at heart an affective art, so monitoring your responses to characters is a necessary thing to do while reading stories and watching plays. In *The Lion, the Witch and the Wardrobe*, Lewis's carefully drawn characters touch our hearts in a wide variety of ways (e.g., anger, pity, fear, admiration) and as a result elicit many different responses within us as the story unfolds.

ᏫᎿ *For Reflection or Discussion*

The characterization of the four siblings can be pursued in a range of directions:

- You can go back to the second page of the book and chart the progressively negative characterization of Edmund from that point. There are good reasons he is the character whom readers love to hate. As this negative portrait unfolds, ponder how this is important to the design of the story and its religious meaning.

- Lucy was designed by Lewis as a foil to Edmund, whose negative characterization sets off Lucy's positive portrayal. You can chart Lucy's characterization (her traits and actions) from the beginning of the story to the end. What did the author intend to embody in this perennial favorite among the four children?

- Peter and Susan, being less charismatic as characters (though Peter will have his moments before the story is over), are themselves foils to the two dominant siblings. That is, they are attendant characters who are important to the action but lack the depth of characterization of the other two.

- Finally, as we read about the four siblings, we are continuously reminded that this is a children's story. One of the features of this genre is that children want the leading characters to be children with whom they can identify. You may want to explore the ways in which the four siblings—often squabbling and sometimes harmonious—embody universal family experiences.

EDMUND'S INITIATION INTO NARNIA

The second item of business in chapter 3, after the shaming of Lucy, is the entry of Edmund into Narnia via the wardrobe. Even here the technique of the foil is important, as seen, for example, in Lucy's remembering not to close the door of the wardrobe behind her, while Edmund shuts the door, "forgetting what a very foolish thing this is to do" (*LWW*, ch. 3, p. 28). Also important for the emerging picture of Edmund is the suspense we now feel as we wonder how Edmund will deal with the proof he now possesses that Lucy spoke the truth about Narnia.

Chapter 3 records the second entry into Narnia in the story, and it will be followed by yet another, when all four children enter Narnia together. Edmund's entry into Narnia invites comparison with Lucy's earlier entry. A good analytic grid is to treat the first two entries into Narnia as foils—parallels with similarities and differences. Lewis himself once stated the principle that we can apply here. In explaining how the Bible's verse form of parallelism works, Lewis talked about "the same in the other" as a basic principle of art. Thus we need to look for *commonalities* when we are comparing these two entrances, as well as the ways in which Lucy's first experience in Narnia *differs* from what Edmund encounters.

"The principle of art has been defined by someone as 'the same in the other.'
Thus in a country dance you take three steps and then three steps again.
That is the same. But the first three are to the right and the second three to the left.
That is the other. In a building there may be a wing on one side
and a wing on the other, but both of the same shape."

C. S. LEWIS, REFLECTIONS ON THE PSALMS

It is easy to see how Edmund's entry into Narnia resembles Lucy's in chapters 1-2. Here are some common ingredients:

- entry into the wardrobe
- passage through the wardrobe
- entry into a forest
- first sensations, including the crunching of snow underfoot
- encounter with residents of Narnia who happen to be passing by

After we have absorbed these common ingredients, we can analyze the differences. The most important of these is the stark contrast between the two chief personages that the respective siblings meet—Mr. Tumnus versus the White Witch. No wonder Lucy and Edmund have such different views of what is really happening in Narnia. Or perhaps, are the good and bad figures that Lucy and Edumund respectively meet reflections of their own differing characters?

ᘓ *For Reflection or Discussion*

- First you can fill in the details of the similarities noted above. Then move on to the more significant half of the equation: how Lucy and Edmund have opposite experiences in Narnia.
- What do you make of the fact that Lucy meets a wonderful creature of natural virtue, while Edmund meets the most sinister character in the entire story?
- How does the physical description of the White Witch already hint at her moral and spiritual depravity?
- How does the behavior of the Witch reinforce this negative characterization?

THE CHARACTERIZATION OF THE WHITE WITCH

There can be little doubt that the White Witch is one of the triumphs among C. S. Lewis's character creations. She is a sinister figure who grips our emotions and contributes a great deal to the plot, in terms of generating both fear (during her time of tyranny over an entire land) and relief (as she is gradually defeated by Aslan). Here are things that we need to understand about the White Witch:

- There are ways in which the White Witch, for all of her great powers, still resembles a "human." She is human in form, and she fills the recognizably human role of queen. But in spite of this resemblance in form and function, it is also important to remember Mr. Beaver's description of her lineage:

"There isn't a drop of real human blood in the Witch" (*LWW,* ch. 8, p. 81).

• Further, the Witch is a mythical figure, more than "human." She has power to make it always winter and never Christmas in Narnia. Later in the story she enters into negotiations with Aslan, who is himself a figure of transcendent authority and strength, thereby reinforcing our impression of the Witch as a figure of cosmic power. Even to identify her as a witch (the White Witch, with initial capital letters) hints at a supernatural dimension.

4
Turkish Delight
Archetypes

♛

Archetypes are recurrent patterns in literature and in life. These patterns can be images (such as light and darkness), character types (such as the hero and the trickster) or plot motifs (such as the quest and the initiation). These recurrent patterns are the building blocks of the literary imagination. Writers could not avoid using them if they tried.

Archetypes are a universal language. We know what they mean simply by virtue of being humans in this world. We all know experiences of winter and hunger, sibling rivalry and tyrannical bullies. One scholar speaks of archetypes as "any of the immemorial patterns of response to the human situation in its most permanent aspects."

The first three chapters of *The Lion, the Witch and the Wardrobe* have already featured a host of archetypes: sibling rivalry, the creepy country house, winter, the cozy home (Mr. Tumnus's cave), the sinister forest, the wicked witch. It is a rare page of the book where we cannot catch at least a glimpse of some literary archetype.

"Answering the question 'How should the Chronicles of Narnia be read?' involves coming to grips with the term 'archetype.' Formidable as the word sounds, its dictionary meaning is simply a model, an example of a type or group. . . . Writers in all ages have used gardens, calm, festivity, and harvest, for example, as symbols of desirable states of being and deserts, storms, discord, and drought as corresponding symbols of undesirable conditions; and they have used the hero, the benevolent king, and the wise older guide as good characters, while the villain, the tyrant, and the witch appear again and again as the corresponding evil figure."

PETER J. SCHAKEL, *READING WITH THE HEART*

Lewis was well aware of archetypes. In *A Preface to Paradise Lost,* Lewis calls the recurrent images and motifs (patterns) of literature "stock themes" as well as "archetype[s]" and "archetypal patterns." The power of these recurrent patterns is that they embody universal human experience to an unusual degree. In the words of Lewis, "giants, dragons, paradises, gods, and the like are themselves the expression of certain basic elements in man's spiritual experience." In connection with one of his favorite authors, Edmund Spenser, Lewis claimed that "Spenser's symbols embody not simply his own experience, nor that of his characters at a given moment, but the experience of the ages." (Lewis's own book entitled *Spenser's Images of Life* is an example of archetypal criticism.)

ᯡ *For Reflection or Discussion*

The uses of an archetypal approach to the Narnian books are multiple, and they include the following:

- Identifying archetypes is useful in showing the unity of a story. The moment you identify the forest in the early chapters of *The Lion, the Witch and the Wardrobe* as the sinister forest with supernatural properties, details suddenly fall into place. The organizing potential of archetypes like the journey to a strange world or the temptation motif is unlimited.

- Archetypes are part of what psychologists (and Lewis) call *the racial* or *collective unconscious*. Lewis called them "stock responses." This is simply a way of saying that archetypes evoke universal and deeply seated human emotions and responses. Identifying and then pondering the archetypes in *The Lion, the Witch and the Wardrobe* is a way of reading with the heart, allowing an affective level of response to become active.

- The moment you identify archetypes in a specific story, you begin to remember examples of the same archetypes in other works of literature that you have read. These memories and connections, in turn, can amplify and add depth of field to your experience of *The Lion, the Witch and the Wardrobe*. The more connections you draw, the richer will be your experience. As Northrop Frye, the foremost archetypal critic, puts it, "All themes and characters and stories that you encounter in literature belong to one big interlocking family. . . . You keep associating your literary experiences together: you're always being reminded of some other story you read or movie you saw or character that impressed you."

- Archetypes are a chief avenue by which literature intersects with the Bible. The Bible itself is a book of archetypes (for more on this, see *Dictionary of Biblical Imagery*, edited by Leland Ryken, James C. Wilhoit and Tremper Longman III), and a very fruitful two-way street can be set up between the Bible and literature by means of archetypes.

- Finally, archetypes are present in literature because they are present in life. Exploring the archetypes of Lewis's book is thus one of the best ways of relating the book to your own life and observations.

THE WHITE WITCH AS ARCHETYPE

It will be important to apply what has been said about archetypes at every point in the story, though the cumulative weight of the archetypes makes them increasingly important as the story unfolds. For the moment, it is our task to use archetypal criticism as a lens by which to see what is happening in Edmund's encounter with Turkish Delight.

Let's start with the Witch. There is another feature of archetypes in addition to what was stated above. Often it is possible to trace an archetype back to an original prototype—an ancient model of which subsequent examples seem to be variations. For example, the fall from innocence reverberates throughout literature, but the story where we see the pattern in its full essence is the story of Adam and Eve in Genesis 3.

Lewis himself clues us into what he intended with the White Witch as an archetype. In a letter, Lewis wrote that "the Witch is of course Circe, . . . because she is . . . the same Archetype we find in so many fairy tales. No good asking where any individual author got *that*. We are born knowing the Witch, aren't we?" Circe is the mythical original of a temptress who transformed men into animals by getting them to drink her magical potion. If we trace her through the fairy tale genre mentioned by Lewis, we can add to the mix such examples as the witch who caught Hansel and Gretel and the Wicked Witch of the West in *The Wizard of Oz*—evil beings beyond the ordinary human experience, and significantly, beings who hate children. Thus Lewis is underscoring the universal knowledge of such creatures that we all share: we don't need to be taught about what the Witch is really like, for we have already encountered her many times in our life and reading. As Lewis puts it, we are "born knowing the Witch." This shared familiarity speaks to the *universal* nature of an archetype.

ᥰ *For Reflection or Discussion*

With the archetypal identity of the White Witch established, you can start fitting the details in chapter 4 around that pattern. The archetype becomes a lens that allows you to see how things fit together, in the process alerting you to nuances that you might otherwise miss.

CHAPTER 4 AS A TEMPTATION STORY

The White Witch is an archetypal *character type*. The *plot motif* that governs the famous "Turkish Delight" chapter is the temptation. When reading a temptation story, we do well to pay attention to three things: (1) the agent of temptation, (2) the victim of the temptation and (3) the process by which the tempter or temptress manipulates the victim and gradually comes to dominate the victim. Paying attention to these three ingredients will pay dividends with chapter 4.

The chief trait of a tempter or temptress is cleverness or craftiness (just as in the story of the Fall in Genesis 3:1, where we are told that "the serpent was more crafty than any other beast of the field that the LORD God had made"). Usually a major part of the craftiness of a temptress is her ability to deceive her victim.

The victim in a temptation story is usually characterized above all by gullibility. Therein lies part of the hold that such stories have over us: as readers we can hardly believe that the victim is giving in to the temptation. We want to stop the character but are powerless to do so. The more we want to warn a victim who needs our help but is beyond our reach, the more completely we too feel ourselves to be under the control of the White Witch.

As for the process by which Edmund succumbs to the temptation, it all has to do with his inability to control his taste for a candy called Turkish delight. The more Edmund consumes, the further he falls under the control of the White Witch—and the more information he indiscriminately discloses that will bring others under her control as well.

Turkish Delight

The Turkish delight that so ensnares Edmund has its origins in eighteenth-century Turkey during the time of the Ottoman Empire, when sugar was first introduced to Turkish confectioners. This popular sweet, known as *lokum* in Turkey and elsewhere in the East, is primarily made from sugar and starch and often includes small pieces of various nuts (e.g., pistachio, hazelnut or almond), as well as flavorings such as rosewater, lemon or other fruits. The popular legend says that this "sweet" (as the British term it) was created at the request of a sultan who wished to please his many wives by offering them a unique new dessert. This delicately scented and sugary-sweet candy was first exported to the West in the nineteenth century by a British traveler, who renamed it Turkish delight. In Lewis's childhood, it would have traditionally been offered as a special Christmas treat. Most Americans find Turkish delight distasteful and regard Edmund's overwhelming attraction to it as just another evidence of his deepening corruption.

ᥱ *For Reflection or Discussion*

The foregoing grid of the temptation story is a marvelous guide to organize your perceptions of chapter 4.

- Collect the evidence that the White Witch is a master temptress, including the things that she offers to Edmund to entice him.
- When you turn the spotlight on Edmund, observe the ways he is a gullible victim. Note the specific undesirable traits he displays as he pursues his ignominious career as the Witch's dupe.
- You can also trace how the ongoing sequence of events (the plot) fits the pattern of growing mastery of the temptress over her victim. In this regard, pay attention to Edmund's behavior when he meets up with Lucy just before their return to the real world (for example, notice how the Witch's deceptiveness is now perpetuated by Edmund's deceptiveness).

RIVAL VIEWS OF NARNIA

After the frightening action of the temptation of Edmund, we return to normalcy at the end of the chapter as Lucy and Edmund meet each other following their respective sojourns in Narnia. As so often in the story, Lucy and Edmund are foils to each other, and it is useful to see how this is worked out by the author. There is also an important note of foreshadowing as Lucy and Edmund speak at cross-purposes regarding what Narnia is like. Because these two siblings have met and been influenced by such opposing characters in the strange world of Narnia, their responses to Narnia are also opposed. What is true about Narnia is exactly the question that will dominate the next chapter of the book.

5

Back on This Side of the Door
How Real Is Narnia?

Rhythm is crucial to storytelling, especially when stories are in written rather than oral form and are divided into chapters. We cannot be kept at a fever pitch of emotional intensity for chapter after chapter. Consciously composed stories like *The Lion, the Witch and the Wardrobe* swing back and forth between the familiar and the unfamiliar, or between one type of action and another, or between action and reflection. Chapter 5 is a reflective chapter that seems short on action but raises a very important issue for the book as a whole.

A summary of the action for the chapter is this: Lucy and Edmund rejoin the game of hide-and-seek that had been going on when they entered Narnia; Edmund betrays Lucy by denying that he has been to Narnia; Peter and

Susan doubt Lucy's sanity and decide to "go and tell the whole thing to the Professor" (LWW, ch. 5, p. 47); in a long dialogue that follows, the Professor leads the children to question their assumption that "other worlds" like Narnia cannot possibly exist; all four children take refuge in the wardrobe when Mrs. Macready comes their way with a group that is touring the house.

The function of this chapter is to bring the question of the nature of reality aggressively into our minds. There are several especially relevant considerations:

- Every piece of fiction, whether realistic or fantastic, raises the question of how a fictional world relates to the real world in which we actually live.
- If a story introduces a fantastic or "other" world into the action, we move to a more intense degree of the question, as we need to consider "what is real" beyond simply the question of fictional reality.
- Because Narnia is given a Christian identity, with qualities of the Christian supernatural intermixed, the question of how the world of this particular fictional and fantastic world is real becomes even more important.

What Constitutes "the Real" in Fiction and Fantasy?

The accusation that fiction is unreal and does not contribute anything truthful to our understanding is perennial, and a lot of literary theory through the centuries has busied itself with replying to the charge. The oldest reply was the classical theory that literature is an imitation (mimesis) of life. A customary term by which this principle is known is verisimilitude—lifelikeness. The ostensible unreality of a story becomes accentuated when it is not simply a work of fiction but a work of fantasy as well. Such a story seems as a result even more escapist than a work of realistic fiction.

The question of reality in fictional and fantastic stories actually has two aspects. One is the kind of reality that exists within stories themselves. Lewis made one of the best comments on the subject when he defended Spenser's fantasy work The Faerie Queene as having "a life of its own," by which he meant that a character or setting is so compelling to our imagination as to

Reality, Reason and Faith

Reason played a significant role in helping C. S. Lewis *come to an understanding of the question of reality. In particular, the teenage Lewis benefited from the logical rigor he was taught by his tutor, W. T. Kirkpatrick. A gifted teacher, Kirkpatrick honed the mind of his brilliant young student, developing within Lewis the ability to quickly and confidently reason through an argument, step by step, to its logical conclusion. In an autobiographical allegory,* The Pilgrim's Regress, *Lewis describes the journey of his main character from unbelief to salvation. Though romantic longing is key in drawing the protagonist toward faith, at a crucial point in the narrative he is rescued from imprisonment by Reason. Indeed, both reason and imagination were essential elements in Lewis's conversion to the Christian faith.*

In tribute to his much-loved tutor, C. S. Lewis fashioned several of his fictional characters after Kirkpatrick: the wise "old" professor in The Lion, the Witch and the Wardrobe, *who is also Digory Kirke in* The Magician's Nephew; *Lord Digory in* The Last Battle; *as well as the character of MacPhee in* That Hideous Strength, *the final volume of his space trilogy.*

seem real to us. Elsewhere, Lewis made the same point when he distinguished between "realism of presentation" and "realism of content." Realism of presentation is "the art of bringing something close to us, making it palpable and vivid, by sharply observed or sharply imagined detail," whereas realism of content means aspects of a story that are "true to life" and thereby seem believable to us.

A second way in which fictional and fantastic stories can be real is that they embody realities that we experience in life. Lifelike in this case means *truthful to human experience.* The painter Pablo Picasso once said, "We all know

"The word 'lifelike' as applied to literature is ambiguous.
It may mean 'like life as we know it in the real world';
in that sense the dullest character in a realistic novel may be 'lifelike,'
i.e. he is very like some real people and as lifeless as they.
On the other hand 'lifelike' may mean 'seeming to have a life of its own';
in that sense Captain Ahab, old Karamazov, Caliban, Bre'er Rabbit, and
the giant who says 'fee-fi-fo-fum' in Jack the Giant-Killer, are all lifelike.
Whether we have met anything like them in the real world is irrelevant."

C. S. LEWIS, *STUDIES IN MEDIEVAL AND RENAISSANCE LITERATURE*

that Art is not [literal] truth. Art is a lie that makes us realize truth." Or as eighteenth-century man of letters Samuel Johnson put it, details in fictional stories are "not . . . mistaken for realities, but . . . they bring realities to mind."

ℭℯ *For Reflection or Discussion*

The two types of reality mentioned above can be applied to *The Lion, the Witch and the Wardrobe* in the following ways:

- The notion that the imaginary characters, places and events of the Narnian stories take on a life of their own is something that your own love of the descriptive details in the story can validate. Which specifics in *The Lion, the Witch and the Wardrobe* have this quality for you?
- Both the realistic fictional framework of the Narnian stories (the children pictured as living in the big house in the British countryside) and the far-flung fantasies of Narnia itself are real in the sense of being, at the level of human experiences and inner principles, like life as we know it. Reflecting on ways in which *The Lion, the Witch and the Wardrobe* is true to your own experiences is essential to a full experience of the story. Remember that archetypes are one of the ways in which literature intersects with life.

The Role of Christian Apologetics

With questions like the above in mind, you can see what is going on in the dialogue that dominates chapter 5. The impulse of Peter and Susan is to believe that Narnia cannot be real. The Professor emerges as the archskeptic—not a skeptic regarding Narnia's existence but regarding the siblings' blithe assumption that other worlds do not exist. The Professor is the archetypal sage or wise man in this conversation—the possessor of true knowledge. You can explore how this works itself out in the actual exchange between the Professor and his questioners.

But more is going on here than simply literary questions of fictional reality and the truthfulness of fantasy. Narnia is at one level the world of the Christian supernatural—a transcendent spiritual reality that surrounds us at every moment, though it is undetected by our physical senses. So at a deeper level, the dialogue that occupies most of chapter 5 is really raising what in Christian apologetics is known as the question of evidence. In the story itself, the uncertainty that needs to be resolved is whether or not Narnia is real, as reported by Lucy. However, for us as readers, this question takes on the added dimension of whether we believe in the existence of spiritual realities in our own world. In other words, is there proof that the Christian supernatural exists, and is it true as it has been reported to us by Scripture and Christian theology?

For Reflection or Discussion

To pursue this line of inquiry will take you into the realm of religion, and good questions to consider include the following:

- How does Peter and Susan's knee-jerk rejection of the possibility of other worlds epitomize both the modern spirit and the unbelieving mind in any age?
- How does the Professor's line of reasoning with the children represent an incipient Christian apologetic for the existence of the supernatural?

"We have to take reality as it comes to us. . . .
Though I cannot see why [the Christian faith] should be so,
I can tell you why I believe it is so. I have explained why I have to believe
that Jesus was (and is) God. . . . I believe it on His authority.
Do not be scared by the word authority.
Believing things on authority only means believing them because
you have been told them by someone you think trustworthy.
Ninety-nine per cent of the things you believe are believed on authority."

C. S. LEWIS, MERE CHRISTIANITY

6

Into the Forest
Worldmaking and the Storyteller's Art

Setting is the forgotten element in many people's analysis of stories. This is a great loss, since settings are interesting to explore and contribute significantly to stories. The concept of setting in narrative is a great deal more complex than many readers realize. Settings can be physical, temporal and cultural. Their functions are multiple:

- Settings serve as a "container" for the actions and agents that operate within them. We can profitably think in terms of a correspondence between a given setting and the events and characters that exist within it.

- Settings are part of the concrete vividness of a story—a means by which the story comes alive in our imagination.

- Settings can contribute atmosphere to a story (a quality, incidentally, that C. S. Lewis greatly admired).
- Settings usually take on symbolic meanings (at the very least being positive or negative in connotation).

"The Three Musketeers makes no appeal to me at all.
The total lack of atmosphere repels me. There is no country in the book—
save as a storehouse of inns and ambushes. There is no weather.
When they cross to London there is no feeling that London differs from Paris. . . .
It is here that Homer shows his supreme excellence.
The landing on Circe's island, the sight of the smoke going up from amidst
those unexplored woods, the god meeting us. . . . The peril that lurks here, the silent,
painless, unendurable change into brutality, is worthy of the setting."

C. S. LEWIS, "ON STORIES"

For Reflection or Discussion

This theory on the role of setting in narrative can be applied at any point in your exploration of *The Lion, the Witch and the Wardrobe*. What aspects of the setting of this story particularly appeal to you, make the story come alive, create a world that you enjoy exploring?

THE CONCEPT OF A NARRATIVE WORLD

When storytellers create a story, they at the same time create a whole world having its own distinctive features. Thus identifying the distinguishing features of the world of a story is one of the most crucial things that a reader can do.

While identifying the traits of a story's world is a useful organizing framework for our experience of the story, this activity does more than help to unify our grasp of the story. It is also a part of understanding the worldview of a story. Flannery O'Connor says, "It is from the kind of world the writer creates, from the kind of character and detail he invests it with, that a reader can find *the intellectual meaning* of a book."

How can an imaginary world itself embody the values and themes of a story? Twentieth-century fiction writer Joyce Cary provides the answer: "All writers . . . must have, to compose any kind of story, some picture of the world, and of what is right and wrong in that world." That is, the world a storyteller creates is offered as that author's picture of what really exists (the question of reality) and as the author's commentary on values and morality.

One of the most characteristic gifts of C. S. Lewis as a literary critic was his ability to generalize about the characteristics of the world of a given work of literature. The goal of his book on Spenser's *Faerie Queene* was to help make the reader "an inhabitant of its world." Because Spenser was such a large influence on the Narnian stories, we can see at once the relevance of the traits that Lewis ascribes to Spenser's imaginary fairy land: it is a world of "quests and wanderings and inextinguishable desires." A similar relevance can be seen in Lewis' description of the world of Kenneth Grahame's *The Wind in the Willows*, a fantasy story with animal characters: "The happiness which [*The Wind in the Willows*] presents to us is in fact full of the simplest and most attainable things—food, sleep, exercise, friendship, the face of nature, even (in a sense) religion."

ॐ *For Reflection or Discussion*

Any final attempt to codify the features of the imagined world of *The Lion, the Witch and the Wardrobe* must wait until one has finished the book. But at any point in the story it is useful to make conscious statements about the world that Lewis has created, on the understanding that this is the author's picture of (a) what really exists, (b) what is of most value in the world and (c) what constitutes good and evil in the world.

ENTERING NARNIA A THIRD TIME

There is an incremental (growth) principle at work in the successive entries that various of the children make into Narnia in this book—and we might note in passing the folktale principle of threefold repetition. You might wish to ponder how the three entries are similar and dissimilar and what makes the third entry climactic.

This is also a good time to take stock of how the transition between the real world and the strange world (in this case Narnia) requires inventiveness on the storyteller's part. Within a given story, trips into the other world cannot be so numerous as to become commonplace. Nor can they simply be duplicates of each other. They must also be interesting in themselves.

Most of the fairy stories "that do not just tell us about the world of the fairy tale in and of itself but tell us something about where it is located and how to reach it . . . seem to agree that it is not as far away as we might think and under the right circumstances not really all that hard to get to. . . . In each case, a strange world opens up when it chooses to open up."

FREDERICK BUECHNER, *TELLING THE TRUTH*

"A TERRIBLE SURPRISE": CHAPTER 6 AS A HORROR STORY

Once the children enter the forest, the chapter becomes a dark adventure story. It is governed by the journey motif, but of a very troubling sort. Lucy guides the party to Mr. Tumnus's cave, where they find the place ransacked and a threatening note from the captain of the secret police posted. The children subsequently travel aimlessly through the woods, and the chapter ends as they acknowledge that they haven't "the least idea of the way home from here" (*LWW*, ch. 6, p. 62). The archetype of the children lost in the woods casts its shadow over the action. It is true that a helpful robin serves as a guide, but the children decide that they have no way of knowing whether the robin is leading them into a trap.

Entering Narnia

Here is how C. S. Lewis chose to describe the moments of transition from his fictional "real world" to Narnia in his other six stories:

- Prince Caspian (*1950*). *The four children (Peter, Susan, Edmund and Lucy) are pulled abruptly back into Narnia when Prince Caspian blows Susan's ivory Horn in a moment of need.*

- The Voyage of the "Dawn Treader" (*1952*). *Lucy, Edmund and Eustace enter Narnia by way of a painting that suddenly comes to life.*

- The Silver Chair (*1953*). *Eustace and Jill ask Aslan for help and then find an unlocked door in a garden wall that leads them into Narnia.*

- The Horse and His Boy (*1954*). *This is the one Narnian tale that does not have a transition into Narnia, as the story takes place during the years when the four children (Peter, Susan, Edmund and Lucy) reign as kings and queens over the inhabitants of Narnia. That is, the action of this tale occurs during the final few pages of The Lion, the Witch and the Wardrobe. (See chapter 11 of C. S. Lewis: A Biography by Roger Lancelyn Green and Walter Hooper for a helpful chronology that illustrates how English time intersects with Narnian time. Readers should also be aware that during the span of the seven Narnian books, there are 2,555 Narnian years to only 52 English or Earth years.)*

- The Magician's Nephew (*1955*). *In this story about the origins of Narnia, a magician uses trickery and magic rings to send two children, Polly and Digory, into other worlds, in one of which they witness the creation of Narnia.*

- The Last Battle (*1956*). *In this final story in the Narnian chronicles, seven friends of Narnia, children from the earlier stories, are thrust suddenly back into Narnia as the result of a train wreck in England.*

In an essay entitled "On Fairy-Stories," J. R. R. Tolkien gives us a very helpful formula for fairy stories when he identifies the central action as adventures "in the Perilous Realm." In this chapter, the children have indeed begun adventures in the "Perilous Realm" of Narnia.

> ### ◔ *For Reflection or Discussion*
> You can make sense of the unfolding action by noting how many of
> the details add to a building anxiety and sense of danger. It is a uni-
> versal rule of storytelling that things get worse before they get better.
> A literary critic once used the formula "design for terror" to describe
> action such as transpires in this chapter.

7

A Day with the Beavers
The Good Place Motif

We enter chapter 7 at a point of high tension—with the four children lost
in a very big woods. The robin who had guided them disappears, but they
immediately encounter a beaver who quickly emerges as a kindly authority
figure and caretaker. He establishes credentials (Lucy's handkerchief, which
has been passed from Mr. Tumnus) that make him trustworthy, and we even
hear about how "Aslan is on the move" (*LWW*, ch. 7, p. 67).

Overshadowing everything else, though, is the sumptuous feast that everyone enjoys in the domestic utopia represented by the home of Mr. and
Mrs. Beaver. Both as a reader and as an author, Lewis appreciated the quality
of "homeliness" within a story. This is readily evident in this scene in the Beavers' cozy home as well as in the earlier description of Mr. Tumnus's snug
cave. In both of them we can clearly see Lewis's great enjoyment of and appreciation for simple everyday pleasures.

Before we explore the mouthwatering details, we should take time to note
the literary lineage of the peaceful interlude as a motif in serious narrative

literature (especially epic and romance). It is a convention that the hero engaged on a quest of great importance experiences a temporary lull in his dangerous mission by being entertained in a peaceful domestic haven, usually in a rural or pastoral setting.

The title of chapter 7 speaks of the children's spending "*a day* with the Beavers," and even this has a literary significance. A subgenre within pastoral literature is the ideal day. Such literature lovingly catalogs the activities and pleasures of a typical day in the life of characters living in a particular locale. Psalm 23 belongs to this tradition, describing the typical events in a good shepherd's daily routine, as seen from the viewpoint of the sheep who are recipients of the shepherd's ideal provision.

Lewis notes "the presence [in children's stories] of beings other than human which yet behave, in varying degrees, humanly: the giants and dwarfs and talking beasts. I believe these to be at least (for they may have many other sources of power and beauty) an admirable hieroglyphic which conveys psychology, types of character, more briefly than novelistic presentation and to readers whom novelistic presentation could not yet reach. . . . The child who has once met [Kenneth Grahame's] Mr Badger has ever afterwards, in its bones, a knowledge of humanity and of English social history which it could not get in any other way."

"ON THREE WAYS OF WRITING FOR CHILDREN"

What goes on at the "very snug little home" (*LWW*, ch. 7, p. 73) of Mr. and Mrs. Beaver has literary roots broader than the epic/romance interlude. It is in the nature of literature to give us two worlds—an ideal world and unideal world, dream and nightmare, good place and bad place. Chapter 7 looks at just one of these, even though as we absorb it we are conscious of a surrounding context of danger. (Your first impulse may actually be to doubt that this chapter is devoted entirely to idealized experience, though you can prove to your satisfaction that this is the case.)

"Sometimes, as in the happy endings of comedies, or in the ideal world of romances, we seem to be looking at a pleasanter world than we ordinarily know. Sometimes, as in tragedy and satire, we seem to be looking at a world more devoted to suffering or absurdity than we ordinarily know. In literature we always seem to be looking either up or down. . . . There are two halves to literary experience, then. Imagination gives us both a better and a worse world than the one we usually live with, and demands that we keep looking steadily at them both."

NORTHROP FRYE, *THE EDUCATED IMAGINATION*

If the good place motif is thus important in literature generally (including the Bible), this gets elevated to a whole new level when we come to children's literature. Children absolutely love creature comforts, especially those involving enclosed spaces and food, and authors and illustrators of children's literature lavishly indulge the urge for images of such comforts. In fact, it is easy to parody the detailed lists of pleasantries in children's literature, as the following passage does: "Once upon a time, a very very very *long* time ago (*ever* so long ago), a teeny tiny weeny furry bear (smaller than most) named Norbert Smythe lived with a great many other teeny tiny weeny furry bears in a cozy cave lined with cupboards filled with honey jars and jam tarts and other yummy gooey treats fixed by Norbert's mummy." (Norbert, incidentally, lived "in the middle, the absolute center, of a great big huge *enormous* forest.")

For Reflection or Discussion

Dip into your memory for instances of the peaceful interlude in stories you have read.

- Think about the intention and/or effect of allowing the children on a dangerous mission to enjoy an interlude that totally absorbs them in pleasures of the moment, free from anxiety about the tests that await them.

- Scrutinize the entire chapter (not just the account of the meal) under the rubric of "good news for frightened children."
- Homes in literature (and usually in life) are an extension of personality. Explore how the domestic residence and routine of the Beavers contribute to their characterization. What makes Mr. and Mrs. Beaver such attractive and memorable characters?
- Try to look at the home and feast through a child's eyes and consider why Lewis selected the specific details that we find in the account. Interacting with children on this subject might prove interesting.
- One of the functions of literature is to arouse longings. Usually individual parts of a book do this, but sometimes it is an overall effect of the book as well. Pay attention to the longings that arise in you at various points in your progress through *The Lion, the Witch and the Wardrobe.*

8

What Happened After Dinner
Images of Good

Literary critics speak gravely about "the notorious problem of portraying the good," and even C. S. Lewis, writing about John Milton's Satan, theorized that authors find it easier to create evil characters than good ones. The problem has been greatly exaggerated, and Lewis actually found no difficulty in making the good attractive in his fiction.

Before exploring the particular images of the good in *The Lion, the Witch and the Wardrobe,* we should note how important to the literary enterprise the portrayal of good and evil is. Someone who made a detailed study of how stories embody their moral viewpoints concluded that the final effect of a story "depended heavily on how successful its creator was in controlling our sympathy and antipathy toward, our approval and disapproval of, characters, thoughts, and actions." Accordingly, storytellers who aim at a wholesome effect lavish much of their technique on making the good attractive and the evil ultimately unattractive. Indeed, J. R. R. Tolkien found "alarming" a literary situation in which "goodness is bereft of its proper beauty."

For Reflection or Discussion

The general principle that writers secure their effect by making the good attractive to the reader and the evil ultimately repulsive (after deceptive appearances have been stripped away) is one that you can confirm from your own reading. What are your most powerful literary images of the good? Rereading some favorite passages would provide a good context for assimilating C. S. Lewis's images of the good.

CATEGORIES OF THE GOOD

In his analysis of Edmund Spenser's "images of life" (that is, life in both its good and bad aspects), Lewis arranges Spenser's images of good and evil into categories. The "image of good" in *The Faerie Queene* yields these categories:

- the veiled and mysterious quality of good
- natural good (including the humble and rustic)
- order, ceremony and formality (often linked with rulership)
- spontaneous, life-giving energy

This grid bears some general similarities to the archetypes and image patterns for the good in *The Lion, the Witch and the Wardrobe*. Here are some categories, accompanied by arbitrarily chosen examples (all taken from chapter 8):

- children and the childlike as images of good: Lucy, Peter and Susan
- images of natural and humble virtue, especially as represented by nonhuman residents of Narnia (Mr. and Mrs. Beaver)
- images associated with kingship and its formalities: Aslan as king; the formal titles by which the four children are called (e.g., "Daughter of Eve"); the castle of Cair Paravel

ᜃ For Reflection or Discussion

Try tracing these clusters of images backward into the earlier parts of the book and forward as the book continues to unfold.

In reply to the claim that children should not be exposed to the terrors pictured in fairy stories: "In the fairy tales, side by side with the terrible figures, we find the immemorial comforters and protectors, the radiant ones."

C. S. LEWIS, "ON THREE WAYS OF WRITING FOR CHILDREN"

ASLAN AS SUPREME IMAGE OF THE GOOD

The dominant subject of chapter 8 is Aslan, who is introduced into the story in full-fledged manner for the first time. He does not actually enter the action as a character yet, but he is discussed at length by Mr. Beaver. This is actually a "trick of the trade" among storytellers and is known as the delayed entrance of the hero. It creates a sense of anticipation, so that when the hero finally makes an actual appearance, we are already won over.

The most important thing about Aslan—the element that can't be missed—is that he is given qualities of Christ and performs acts that correspond to the redemptive actions of Christ. Wherever these allusions and correspondences come into your consciousness as you read, you should embrace them and not suppress them. They are an intended part of the meaning of the story.

Having said that, we need to respect what Lewis himself said about his creation (perhaps *discovery* is a better word) of Aslan. Here are three relevant considerations:

- Lewis himself did not regard Aslan as an allegorical figure: "By an allegory I mean a composition (whether pictorial or literary) in which immaterial realities are represented by feigned physical objects. . . . If Aslan represented the immaterial Deity in the same way in which Giant Despair represents Despair, he would be an allegorical figure." In other words, Lewis raises the possibility of allegorical connections, only to deny it.

- Aslan was, however, conceived by Lewis as corresponding in the world of Narnia to Christ in the world of Palestine; Aslan was "an invention giving an imaginary answer to the question, 'What might Christ become like, if there really were a world like Narnia and He chose to be incarnate and die and rise again in *that* world as he actually has done in ours?' This is not allegory at all. . . . The Incarnation of Christ in another world is mere supposal: but *granted* the supposition, He would really have been a physical object in that world as He was in Palestine."

- The creation of Aslan did not begin with an intention to create a Christ-figure but with the usual process of literary creation: "Some people seem to think that I began by asking myself how I could say something about Christianity to children; then fixed on the fairy tale as an instrument; then . . . drew up a list of basic Christian truths and hammered out 'allegories' to embody them. This is all pure moonshine. I couldn't write in that way at all. Everything began with images. . . . At first there wasn't even anything Christian about them; that element pushed itself in of its own accord."

To truly understand how Lewis viewed the character of Aslan in his Narnian stories, then, we must be very clear about the distinction between an allegorical approach and what we might term Lewis's concept of *supposal*. As Lewis explained in a letter to a class of American fifth-graders:

You are mistaken when you think that everything in the books "represents" something in this world. Things do that in *The Pilgrim's Progress* but I'm not writing in that way. I did not say to myself "Let us represent Jesus as He really is in our world by a Lion in Narnia": I said "Let us *suppose* that there were a land like Narnia and that the Son of God, as He became a Man in our world, became a Lion there, and then imagine what would happen." If you think about it, you will see that it is quite a different thing.

While there are allegorical correlations between the character of Aslan and the figure of Christ, the story itself can be trusted to signal where the relevant parallels exist. To allegorize the story to make virtually all details correspond to something in the life of Christ would violate Lewis's intention and also the normal way in which we use language. We need to begin by accepting Aslan first of all as an animal character in a fantasy story. Symbolic meanings must be allowed to emerge naturally from this imagined character and must not be imposed by an external framework that requires every detail in the story to yield a christological meaning.

Lewis viewed allegory as limiting because allegory is dependent on what the author already knows, while in a mythic (nonallegorical) approach a story may well communicate truths that are beyond the author's own apprehension. In other words, in the character of Aslan there are elements of truth that go beyond our intellectual comprehension and that speak directly and powerfully to our imagination.

In view of this, we can see how crucial it is that adult readers (whether parents or teachers) not impose an understanding of Aslan's identity prematurely on a young reader's mind. It is inadvisable to preface a reading of *The Lion, the Witch and the Wardrobe* by declaring to a child that Aslan is Jesus. Such an approach unintentionally fails to allow the narrative to speak in an affective way to the imagination of the child. It is far better for children to miss some of the parallels between Aslan and Christ in their first encounter with the book than to have those parallels foisted upon them. Unfortunately, many well-meaning adult readers often violate this crucial restraint. This potential interpretive hazard is aptly illustrated by Philip Ryken's recollection of his first experience with the Narnian stories:

> My own love for the Narnia Chronicles as stories was instant. I can remember the resentment with which I greeted my mother's attempts to see, from time to time, if I was catching the spiritual meanings . . . which lay beneath the surface of the narratives. But I was not about to allow the stories to be ruined by figuring out what they meant.

It is important to allow children to discover the full meaning of Aslan on their own, even if such understanding does not come until years later. The power of the narrative will only be heightened if one trusts the storyteller and allows the story's deeper dimensions to unfold naturally.

A nine-year-old American boy was troubled because he feared that he loved Aslan more than Jesus, and consequently, his mother wrote to C. S. Lewis about his concern. Lewis's reply attempted to reassure his young reader: Laurence "can't really love Aslan more than Jesus, even if he feels that's what he is doing. For the things he loves Aslan for doing or saying are simply the things Jesus really did and said. So that when Laurence thinks he is loving Aslan, he is really loving Jesus: and perhaps loving Him more than he ever did before. Of course there is one thing Aslan has that Jesus has not—I mean, the body of a lion. . . . Now if Laurence is bothered because he finds the lion-body seems nicer to him than the man-body, I don't think he need be bothered at all. God knows all about the way a little boy's imagination works (He made it, after all) and knows that at a certain age the idea of talking and friendly animals is very attractive. So I don't think He minds if Laurence likes the Lion-body."

C. S. LEWIS, *LETTERS TO CHILDREN*

Literary lineages for God as a lion are readily established. To the Western imagination from time immemorial, the lion has been "the king of beasts," a figure of authority. The name Aslan is the Turkish word for lion. Lewis's friend Charles Williams had written a novel entitled *The Place of the Lion*. In the Bible, Christ is "the Lion of the tribe of Judah" (Revelation 5:5). As for the statement in chapter 8, "Wrong will be right, when Aslan comes in sight, / At the sound of his roar" (*LWW*, p. 79), it is reminiscent of the Old Testament prophecy of Amos: "The lion has roared; who will not fear?" (3:8).

An element of the transcendent or numinous becomes part of the reader's experience of Aslan. Within the story itself, the mere mention of Aslan's name brings an experience of the numinous to all those who hear it. "The numinous" in this context should be understood as a simultaneous sense of awe and delight (or horror in the case of those who abhor the Good, as in Edmund's "mysterious horror" [*LWW*, ch. 7, p. 68] at the first mention of the name of Aslan) as the result of being in the presence of something Other, something transcendent and most of all something holy.

In a letter to a young reader, Lewis explained the source for the name of Aslan:
"I found the name in the notes to Lane's *Arabian Nights:*
it is the Turkish for Lion. I pronounce it Ass-lan myself.
And of course I meant the Lion of Judah."

C. S. LEWIS, *LETTERS TO CHILDREN*

For Reflection or Discussion

Lewis's firm declaration that Aslan should be understood to mean the Lion of Judah certainly opens the door to interpreting Aslan in light of Christ as presented in the Bible and Christian theology. Where do the parallels arise naturally for you? (Again, however, keep in mind that this understanding should not be forced upon a reader, particularly when that reader is a child.)

SUSPENSE AND DANGER

While the anticipatory portrayal of Aslan occupies the central part of chapter 8, the last third is dominated by the conventions of the suspense story and story of danger. Edmund emerges as the archetypal traitor when he is discovered missing from the cottage and is presumed to have gone to the White Witch. You can trace the specifics of Lewis's design for fear at the end of the chapter, as well as theorizing about how the extremely negative characterization of Edmund is important to the form and meaning of the book as a whole.

9

In the Witch's House
Images of Evil

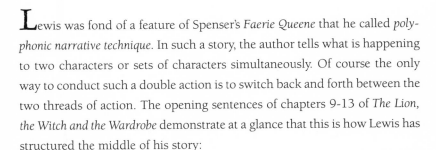

Lewis was fond of a feature of Spenser's *Faerie Queene* that he called *polyphonic narrative technique*. In such a story, the author tells what is happening to two characters or sets of characters simultaneously. Of course the only way to conduct such a double action is to switch back and forth between the two threads of action. The opening sentences of chapters 9-13 of *The Lion, the Witch and the Wardrobe* demonstrate at a glance that this is how Lewis has structured the middle of his story:

- "And now of course you want to know what had happened to Edmund" (*LWW,* ch. 9, p. 88).
- "Now we must go back to Mr. and Mrs. Beaver and the three other children" (*LWW,* ch. 10, p. 100).
- "Edmund meanwhile had been having a most disappointing time" (*LWW,* ch. 11, p. 111).

- "While the dwarf and the White Witch were saying this, miles away the Beavers and the children were walking hour after hour into what seemed a delicious dream" (*LWW,* ch. 12, p. 123).
- "Now we must get back to Edmund" (*LWW,* ch. 13, p. 134).

This technique allows for a great deal of suspense, with a shift to the other story line just when a character is facing a moment of grave danger or uncertainty.

Among stories whose artistic authenticity cannot be questioned we give the highest place precisely to those works which ignore no aspect of man's nature, which confront the most disagreeable aspects of life deliberately and unflinchingly. . . . Reading does not ordinarily represent a flight from life or an attempt to blind oneself to its horrors. . . . The greatest fiction poses these problems in their most essential terms.

SIMON O. LESSER,
FICTION AND THE UNCONSCIOUS

HOW IMAGES OF EVIL ARE IMPORTANT TO STORYTELLING

Good storytellers are as adept at portraying evil as they are at portraying good. For one thing, the essence of a plot is conflict. A plot conflict, moreover, is almost always a variation on the motif of good versus evil. A worthy protagonist in a plot requires a worthy antagonist. In fact, to diminish the sinister qualities of the White Witch in *The Lion, the Witch and the Wardrobe* would be to diminish Aslan, as Lewis perhaps hints by the very title of his book.

But images of evil are important in stories for more than literary reasons. Good literature (as opposed to shallow literature that escapes from life and falsifies it) accurately pictures what we know to be true about reality and human experience. In the world of fallen experience, evil is powerful and pervasive. To do justice to this side of reality, a storyteller needs to create convincing and moving images of evil.

We might assume that fairy stories and children's literature would be exceptions to this rule, but they are not. Authors of such stories do not flinch from creating terrifying images of evil, and children apparently have subconscious intuitions that not only tolerate but desire these images of evil.

This explains why the threat of evil is so relentless at certain points in *The Lion, the Witch and the Wardrobe*. Unless we are already familiar with the story, surely some of the tension strikes us as unexpected in a children's story. The broader view sketched above can help us to understand why the strategy is both necessary and customary in stories.

"I often saw [C. S. Lewis] from the windows of my flat in St. John's Street walking up Bridge Street from Magdalene College [Cambridge]. Once . . . as I opened my front door, he happened to be passing by. With me was my six-year-old daughter, to whom I had just then been reading The Lion, the Witch and the Wardrobe. *A tender-minded child, she was very anxious about Edmund and had asked to go out for a walk as she was finding the story frightening. Lewis stopped to talk with me and I told him what we had been doing. He was most affable. He wore a shabby grey-green overcoat, a battered felt hat, and he carried a knobbly walking stick. His large face was ruddy and cheerful, like a countryman's. No one would have taken him for an academic. When he moved on, courteously raising his hat, I said to my daughter, who had looked at him intently and in silence all through the brief encounter, 'There! that is the very man who wrote the book we've just been reading.' She paused and then said thoughtfully, 'Well, he looks as though he'd make it come all right.'"*

BARBARA REYNOLDS,
"MEMORIES OF C. S. LEWIS IN CAMBRIDGE"

> ### ⁓ For Reflection or Discussion
> Try to remember and take stock of your own encounters with evil in the stories that have mattered most to you. These examples can provide a good context for assimilating Lewis's images of evil.

TYPES OF EVIL IN *THE LION, THE WITCH AND THE WARDROBE*

We can categorize Lewis's images of evil as we did his image patterns for the good. Here is a beginning list, with specimens taken from chapter 9 (dealing with Edmund's arrival at the castle of the White Witch):

- evil humans, known both by their actions and their inner psychology: Edmund is the arch-example, and analyzing the psychological portrait of him in chapter 9 alone will yield much insight
- natural evil: the winter weather and cold that hold Narnia in their grip
- institutional evil: the network of spies and secret police that the White Witch oversees
- supernatural evil: the White Witch, with the most visible evidence of her power in chapter 9 being the creatures' transformation into stone statues

> ### ⁓ For Reflection or Discussion
> The first application of the foregoing framework is to use it as a lens through which to organize the details Lewis puts before you in chapter 9. What particular images and actions here make the White Witch's evil vivid? Then you may want to find examples in the preceding chapters and the following ones.

THE WHITE WITCH AS A FIGURE OF EVIL

The White Witch has been a prominent character in the story all along, and earlier chapters have raised issues of her literary characterization and her identity as a literary archetype. A further way of understanding the Witch is as a figure of evil. The most comprehensive generalization that can be made about her at this level is that she is a *composite figure of evil*.

To begin, even though she is much more than a "human" figure (remember that we were earlier told by Mr. Beaver that "there isn't a drop of real human blood in her" [*LWW*, ch. 9, p. 81]), there are certainly aspects of her character that remind us of people we have known, as well as of evil impulses within ourselves. An obvious instance is how the Witch uses Edmund for her own interests even though she despises him. She is ill-tempered the way some people we know are ill-tempered. She puts on airs about her status as self-declared queen.

And of course the White Witch *is* much more than a "human" figure of evil. It is extending the image too far to regard her as Satan, though her character certainly has demonic aspects. Rather, the White Witch is a personification of the principle of evil in the universe. This is where her supernatural power comes into play: she is much more than simply an evil individual who possesses great power. She calls herself the Queen of Narnia, but her power extends far beyond that of a human queen. The most overt sign of her supernatural evil power is her transformation of living creatures into stone statues. (The background for this is the Roman author Ovid's collection of transformation stories called *The Metamorphoses*.)

ℭ *For Reflection or Discussion*

The White Witch lends herself to exploration as a character along the following lines (but not necessarily only these):

- A large part of her emotional effect on us as readers is the sinister quality she represents and her potential to destroy good characters. Paying attention to our emotions as we read will help us sense her identity as a figure of evil.

- At some moments the White Witch is simply a waspish individual, exhibiting pettiness rather than terrible power. Which are those moments? What do they teach us about the nature of evil?
- As a cosmic or supernatural figure of evil, the Witch is not simply a proud and self-centered nuisance but someone in conflict with Aslan. Locate moments when this is important and reflect on how it expresses part of the religious vision of the book.

10

The Spell Begins to Break
What Readers Like Best in a Story

The point of departure for our analysis of chapter 10 is a comment that C. S. Lewis made in an introduction to one of his favorite English authors (and the one on whom he wrote the most), the sixteenth-century poet Edmund Spenser. Expressing mystification over why Spenser had become known in the twentieth century as "a hard poet [to understand] like Pindar, Donne, or Browning," Lewis writes that until about 1914 *The Faerie Queene* was "a book which spoke at once, like Homer or Shakespeare or Dickens, to every reader's imagination." In other words, Spenser's classic work was both popular and accessible to the general reader.

The idea that there is something that can be called the popular imagination is provocative. We might define the concept of "the popular imagination" as "appealing to the entire cross-section of society, low brow and literati alike."

For Reflection or Discussion

Here are ways to get mileage out of Lewis's suggestion that some authors have a knack for speaking "at once to every reader's imagination":

- Take time to list what you think the human race likes best in a work of literature.
- Having assembled a list of ingredients and general qualities that constitute the "popular imagination," see how the ingredients appear in *The Lion, the Witch and the Wardrobe.*
- Apply the same grid to chapter 10 as a test case: how many of these ingredients or techniques appear in this specimen chapter?

DANGER AND MOMENTARY RELIEF

Chapter 10 is something of a catch-all chapter in the book. The sequence of events is this: Mr. and Mrs. Beaver, Lucy, Peter and Susan make hurried preparations to leave the house and flee for their lives; after trudging through the wintry forest, they enter "an old hiding-place for beavers in bad times" (*LWW,* ch. 10, p. 104); they spend the night in this hole in the bank; at daybreak they hear the sound of jingling bells; when they hear voices, Lucy fears that Mr. Beaver has been captured by the White Witch, but the passing sledge is occupied by Father Christmas, who hands out presents to everyone; Father Christmas departs, and the traveling group goes back into the cave to eat a delicious tea.

The motif of danger unifies most of this chapter's action. The opening action of preparing for a journey from the Beavers' house requires us to reach back to the end of chapter 8, where the group has discovered that Edmund has gone to the Witch, who may be arriving at the house in twenty minutes. When Lucy hears voices, her initial fear that Mr. Beaver has been caught by the Witch is a good indication of how dangerous and frightening the situation has become.

In keeping with what we have said about narrative rhythm, however, even a nightmare chapter like this one encloses the fearful subject matter within a reassuring framework. The danger is mitigated by countercurrents such as the appearance of a kindly parental figure like Father Christmas with his presents, as well as the tea that everyone enjoys in the cave at the very end of the chapter (though the chapter ends with the ominous announcement from Mr. Beaver, "Time to be moving on now" [LWW, ch. 10, p. 110]).

ᏊᎦ For Reflection or Discussion

You can organize what happens in the chapter, as well as your responses to the action, by noting the details that make up the patterns noted above:

- A good organizing framework for assimilating the first half of the chapter is to keep a list of details, large and small, that contribute to the ongoing atmosphere of danger.
- Equally instructive is a list of balancing details that help to mute the anxiety that has been generated by the feeling of menace and threat.

STRATEGIES OF FORESHADOWING

One of the techniques of popular storytelling is to put plenty of foreshadowing into a story to cause us to anticipate future developments and experience the pleasure of fulfillment later in the story. The last third of chapter 10 is filled with foreshadowing.

Father Christmas himself is a foreshadowing. Surely on a first reading his appearance is totally unexpected. He seems stuck into the action. He makes an appearance and then disappears from the story, as though he were some sort of phantom figure. The whole episode is interpolated into the main story, and nothing would be missing from the main action if this episode were omitted.

The real significance of Father Christmas is symbolic, and as a symbol, Father Christmas serves the plot by foreshadowing a number of impending developments. We might note in passing that Lewis's friend Roger L. Green urged Lewis to omit Father Christmas from the story, as he "does not seem to fit quite comfortably into his place," and J. R. R. Tolkien also disliked this addition to the story.

However, if we regard Father Christmas as part of a symbolic design and as serving an important function of foreshadowing at this midway point of the book, things fall into place. In a world where for a long time "it is always winter and never Christmas" (*LWW*, ch. 2, p. 19), the appearance of Father Christmas and his distributing of gifts are the first proof that a great reversal is just around the corner. Further, the particular gifts that Father Christmas gives, along with the specific person whom he designates as the recipient of each present, foreshadow future action.

Ꮽ *For Reflection or Discussion*

- What details make up the symbolism of Father Christmas?
- How do the following presents and their recipients come to fruition later in the story? (If you do not know or remember how the story turns out, you will need to wait for an answer.)

  1. Peter: a shield and armor

  2. Susan: a bow and quiver of arrows and a little ivory horn

  3. Lucy: a little bottle filled with a cordial and a small dagger

  4. Mrs. Beaver: the promise of a new and better sewing machine

  5. Mr. Beaver: the promise that his dam will be finished and mended when he returns home

II

Aslan Is Nearer
The Dynamics of the Plot

We have had occasion to single out characterization and setting in previous chapters, and considerations of plot have entered the discussion. It is time now to address the plot of the story in a formal manner, given that the three ingredients of a story are character, setting and plot.

There can be no doubt that much of the success of *The Lion, the Witch and the Wardrobe* rests with its plot. One reason the magic never ends is that the plot is so masterful. Wherever we turn in the story, we are immersed in an abundance of plot techniques that keep calling attention to themselves if we have developed the antennae by which to notice them. (We can find a small irony here in some of C. S. Lewis's critical essays where he makes somewhat disparaging comments about "reading for the plot.")

---

*"No critics seem to me farther astray than those who deny
that Spenser is an essentially narrative poet.
No one loves him who does not love his story;
outside the proems to the books and cantos he scarcely
writes a line that is not for the story's sake.
His style is to be judged as the style of a story-teller."*

C. S. Lewis,
English Literature in the Sixteenth Century

℘ *For Reflection or Discussion*

The discussion that follows will provide information about the plot of *The Lion, the Witch and the Wardrobe*. Before you read this material, or instead of reading it, you may wish to organize your own thinking about the considerations of plot and action that make Lewis's book the perennial favorite that it is.

THE PLOT OF THE STORY AS A WHOLE

A successful plot encompasses what literary scholars have long called the *architectonics* of the story. This refers to the overriding story as a whole.

Aristotle's *Poetics*—the oldest extant piece of literary theory that we have—remains the starting point for understanding the dynamics of plot. One of the simplest observations that Aristotle made, and one of the most useful, is that a well-constructed plot is a single action having a beginning, a middle and an end. The middle of the story, moreover, must be the logical connection between the beginning and the end.

In this regard *The Lion, the Witch and the Wardrobe* poses a complication by virtue of being a framed story. The central action, consisting of what happens in Narnia, is set within a realistic frame of the four children's lives in the real world before and after they enter Narnia. Many stories are set within an external framework like this, and virtually all journeys to an imaginary land follow this pattern.

If we focus on the story of Narnia as we find it in this book, it is obvious that we enter a larger story at a relatively late point in it. The action of *The Lion, the Witch and the Wardrobe* takes place near the end of the White Witch's stranglehold on Narnia, just before, during and after Aslan's reversal of the effects of evil in the land. There are references, though, to a much larger story with a long history preceding the slice of the action that we encounter in this book. That larger story is a backdrop and does not constitute the plot of *The Lion, the Witch and the Wardrobe*.

We should note, though, that the Narnian books possess to an impressive degree a quality that Lewis praised in Virgil's *Aeneid*. According to Lewis, Virgil wanted to avoid the monotony of "a mere chronicle," that is, a straightforward account of what happened. Virgil's solution, which Lewis called "one of the most important revolutions in the history" of narrative, was to take a single action "and treat it in such a way that we feel the vaster theme to be somehow implicit in it." Lewis does the same in *The Lion, the Witch and the Wardrobe*. The plot itself covers just a few days as judged by our chronology, but we actually conclude the story with a grasp of a very long history of Narnia. We might think in terms of the story's having depth of field (to borrow a concept from photography), always reaching beyond the present action to gesture toward the larger story.

The beginning of the Narnian plot of *The Lion, the Witch and the Wardrobe* is Lucy's encounter with Mr. Tumnus, resulting in his arrest. The prescribed end is the conclusion of a battle and a celebration of victory that includes the coronation of Peter, Susan, Edmund and Lucy. The middle is the events by which we move from one to the other.

This overall plot is governed by a single main conflict, supplemented by secondary ones. The central conflict is the struggle between good and evil for control of Narnia. In its ultimate reaches, this epic spiritual battle is focused on a single combat between the White Witch and Aslan. Of course many other characters and conflicts play their part in this overarching struggle, and it is useful at some point to codify the combats and combatants under the main ones.

A number of smaller conflicts cluster under the central plot conflict of good versus evil. Some of these play themselves out in a relatively short span, while others are present over much of the book. You can profitably compile your own list of subordinate plot conflicts. Here are examples:

- the White Witch's secret police versus a number of characters with whom we as readers strongly sympathize: Mr. Tumnus, Mr. and Mrs. Beaver, Peter, Lucy, Susan

- the villainous Edmund versus his three siblings
- the Witch versus Edmund, once she has gotten the information from him that she needs in order to pursue her evil plans

Stories do not come right out and state their plot conflicts; it takes some analytic thought to identify them. Doing so pays much bigger dividends than most readers think. As you identify plot conflicts, it is useful to know that they might be physical conflicts, character conflicts (including inner conflicts within a person), moral or spiritual conflicts, and supernatural conflicts.

For Reflection or Discussion

Even though we still have nearly half of the story to go in our sequential march through it, this is a good point at which to start codifying your grasp of the overall plot of the story. You can complete this reflection after you finished reading the story.

- Review the first ten chapters and notice the individual plot conflicts that have been introduced and elaborated. Two ways of formulating these conflicts are important—the descriptive (in which you name the agents in conflict, such as Edmund versus Lucy) and the interpretive (in which you probe the deeper principles that are embodied in the externals).
- Peruse these same chapters for references to the larger story of Narnia that reaches back to earlier phases of action.
- Given that it is in the nature of a plot that conflicts move toward resolution, when you have finished reading it will be important to state how the conflicts are finally resolved.

PROGRESSION AS AN INGREDIENT OF PLOT

Chapter 11 is entitled "Aslan Is Nearer." The preceding chapter was entitled "The Spell Begins to Break." These titles hint at the *progression* that is important to a well-managed plot. Part of the architectonics of a story is the controlled change that the storyteller orchestrates as the story unfolds. In a carefully constructed story, we are aware of the changes that are progressively occurring. It begets confidence to see how the storyteller is controlling the flow of action. Lewis praised Milton for his "unremitting *manipulation* of his readers" in *Paradise Lost,* and if we take the time to see how carefully Lewis worked out the progressive element in the unfolding plot of *The Lion, the Witch and the Wardrobe,* we will see that the same quality of careful craftsmanship is present here.

The principle of progression can be seen in microcosm in chapter 11. The protagonist in the action of this chapter is Edmund, as we follow his terrible journey with the wolves and the Witch in their quest to destroy everyone at the Beavers' house and, that failing, to "speed to the Stone Table" (*LWW,* ch. 11, p. 113). But as the journey unfolds, the evil troupe encounters more and more evidence of the growing power of good in the world of Narnia.

ℭ *For Reflection or Discussion*

The element of progression in chapter 11 takes two main forms:

- The relationship between Edmund and the White Witch started as a pretended friendship on the part of the Witch, but it quickly turned into an intense conflict. In chapter 11 you can trace the increasing hostility of the Witch against Edmund and the growing disillusionment of Edmund with the course that he has chosen.

- As the group of terrorists travel through the forest, they (and we with them) encounter more and more signs that good is gradually gaining the ascendancy over evil in Narnia. Trace the ways in which this motif is worked out in chapter 11.

PLOT DEVICES

The skill with which Lewis managed the plot of his Narnian books extends beyond the big picture to the smaller ingredients that contribute to the dynamics of plot. We can experience the effects of these plot devices without consciously noting and naming them, but our enjoyment of what Lewis has achieved can be enhanced if we do notice them. Lewis himself claimed something similar after conducting a close reading of Shakespeare's sonnets: he noted that Shakespeare's skillful structuring of a poem (the equivalent of plot in a story) "of course . . . affects those who have no notion what is affecting them."

"To some, I am afraid, such analysis [of the structure of Shakespeare's sonnets]
will seem trifling, and it is not contended that no man can enjoy the Sonnets
without it any more than that no man can
enjoy a tune without knowing its musical grammar. But unless we are
content to talk simply about the 'magic' of Shakespeare's poetry
(forgetting that magic was a highly formal art) something of the kind is inevitable.
It serves at least to remind us what sort of excellence . . . the Sonnets possess."

C. S. LEWIS, *ENGLISH LITERATURE IN THE SIXTEENTH CENTURY*

The following plot devices that storytellers through the ages have exploited are listed in the order of their frequency in *The Lion, the Witch and the Wardrobe*:

- foreshadowing: hints of future developments or introduction of something that requires further development and resolution
- suspense
- foils: characters, events or situations that "set off" (the literal meaning of *foil*) other characters, events or situations, usually by way of contrast but sometimes by being parallel
- dramatic irony, with readers having superior knowledge to at least some of the characters in the story
- poetic justice: the good rewarded, the bad punished
- surprise

- reversal: an action produces the opposite of its intended effect (as when Edmund thinks he will advance himself by aligning himself with the Witch, only to experience the opposite)

In addition to these plot devices, we should note a major category that does not quite fit under the umbrella of plot devices: archetypal plot motifs. Some common examples include these: quest, ordeal, journey, transformation, death-rebirth, capture, escape, rescue, initiation, temptation, testing and fall from innocence.

> ### ⟨ For Reflection or Discussion
>
> A starting point for sensing how skillfully Lewis manipulated these resources of plot is to focus on chapter 11 and see how many of the plot devices are present there. Then you can start applying the grid to other parts of the story.

12

Peter's First Battle

The Romance Genre

It comes as a jarring surprise to be suddenly immersed in military action (what literary critics call the martial theme) in chapter 12. After all, the story thus far has been governed by the conventions of the fairy tale, the beast fable (a story with animal characters) and the children's fantasy story. But as chapter 12 unfolds, we are plunged into a very different type of story—one of pitched battle in which soldiers kill each other with weapons.

At this point we realize that yet another genre has entered the encyclopedic work that we are reading. A great virtue of the multiplicity of design of this book is the sheer variety that we experience in just 189 pages. But it also requires that we shift gears at times and bring a whole additional set of expectations into play.

The ancient genre of romance does not denote a love story. Many romances have included a romantic love interest, but that is not how we are using the term here. The romance genre is an old genre, sharing certain primitive, simple or naive qualities with the fairy tale, beast fable and children's story. Remember that C. S. Lewis was a specialist in medieval and Renaissance literature, eras when romance was the dominant type of story. The best-known English romance is Edmund Spenser's *The Faerie Queene,* whose influence on the Narnian books is everywhere in evidence, as we have already noted.

The old romances are fantasy stories that often incorporate elements of myth. Supernatural characters and marvelous (more than earthly or human) events are a staple, commonly taking the form of characters' use of magic. The customary setting for romance action is twofold—a forest and a court. In keeping with the courtly setting, the leading characters are aristocratic characters—kings and queens, knights and royal ladies. The storyteller, rather than creating subtle psychological portrayals, motivates the characters by a few basic qualities or ideals, chiefly honor and courage for the men and love and honor for the ladies.

The special ingredient of romance stories is battlefield action as the main story material. In romance stories, *hero* is synonymous with *warrior.* The warrior clad in armor is the most common picture that emerges as we read. The story of this warrior is replete with details of weapons and battlefield strategy.

ℰ *For Reflection or Discussion*

If you wish to take the time, the foregoing description of the romance genre provides a grid through which you can look at the details of chapter 12.

SERIOUSNESS OF ACTION IN ROMANCE

The moment romance conventions enter the book in chapter 12, the story is imbued with a new weightiness. The knight is admittedly a boy, Peter, but the events of this chapter belong to a world of adults at the upper end of the social scale, not children who have stumbled into a magical country in a story of children's adventure. This seriousness enters chapter 12 even before we get to the battle at the end of the chapter.

We sense the seriousness of the action most poignantly with the introduction of the Stone Table. Related to that is "a pavilion pitched on one side of the open place" (*LWW*, ch. 12, p. 125). As the scene unfolds before the children and the Beavers (and us), Aslan appears "in the center of a crowd of creatures" (*LWW*, ch. 12, p. 126). The ultimate seriousness comes when the children speak to Aslan. We also become aware of serious political implications to the action when the children see the far-off castle of Cair Paravel, shining in the sunlight.

Although characters from classical mythology like fauns and dwarfs have mingled with the human characters throughout the story, further mythological creatures suddenly cluster in the action now, reinforcing our sense that the story has taken on a deeper gravity than that of fairy stories and children's literature. The cast of characters, along with their classical or medieval origins, includes the following:

- dryads—nymphs (nature deities of a lower order) who inhabit trees and woods
- naiads—nymphs who inhabit streams and fountains
- centaurs: mythical wild creatures having the body of a horse and the head of a man
- a unicorn: a horselike or goatlike creature with a single horn projecting from the middle of its forehead
- a bull with the head of a man (another wild-man creature)
- "a great Dog," possibly a reference to Cerberus, a three-headed dog that guarded the entrance to the infernal regions

- animals with a range of symbolic meanings from antiquity through the Middle Ages: a pelican, an eagle and two leopards

Through the ages of literary history, these mythological and symbolic creatures could have either positive or negative meanings. Here they are all positive, inasmuch as they surround Aslan and are part of his entourage. Their main import seems to be to lend a supernatural aura to Aslan, in terms appropriate to the land of Narnia, where animal characters are significant. There is also an element of enduring universality to this gathering: the good creatures that are clustered before Aslan indicate the historical longevity and continuity converging in this historic moment.

> ### ℭℯ *For Reflection or Discussion*
> We have noted only a few examples of the details that convey the seriousness of action that comes with the emergence of romance conventions at this point in the book. Search chapter 12 for further evidences.

ROMANCE BATTLE

As we near the end of the chapter, the action finally makes good on the title Lewis gave to the chapter—"Peter's First Battle." The battle begins very suddenly as the assembled creatures scatter and Susan is forced to scale a tree with a Wolf ("a huge gray beast" [*LWW,* ch. 12, p. 131]) snapping and snarling at her heels. Peter instinctively rushes at the beast, and a single combat in the romance tradition ensues. Few details are provided, but the summary statement that "everything was blood and heat and hair," followed by the announcement that "a moment later he found that the monster lay dead and he had drawn his sword out of it" (*LWW,* ch. 12, p. 132), is enough to alert us that warfare in this story will not be conducted by the magic-wand principle but by human combat.

This brings us to the element of literary violence in the story. There is not a lot of it, but there is enough to link this story with the literary tradition of realism. Even the ceremonial last action in chapter 12, the knighting of Sir Peter by Aslan, is accompanied by Aslan's command, "Whatever happens, never forget to wipe your sword" (*LWW,* ch. 12, p. 133).

Two literary phenomena converge at this moment. One is the romance convention of military action conducted by flesh-and-blood combatants. The second is the traditional fairy story that incorporates a strand of realism (some modern-day versions sanitize the stories of this "gory" strand). In Charles Perrault's original version of "Little Red Riding Hood," for example, the wolf eats both the grandmother and the little girl. Later retellings of this classic tale (including the one by the Brothers Grimm) have gradually softened this harsh ending, altering it so that both the grandmother and her granddaughter eventually escape from the wolf unharmed (and wiser for the experience).

The writings of Lewis predate the modern dislike for the inclusion of violence in children's literature. Most writers of children's literature do not share the bias against realism, which they regard as an expression of real life and the evil in it. Madeleine L'Engle, for example, argues that when we remove troubling experiences like death from children's literature, the result is "to confuse children and add to their fears." Lewis, while acknowledging that we must protect children from "haunting, disabling, pathological fears," believed that it is unhelpful to children not to do justice to the kind of world that they actually inhabit.

ॐ *For Reflection or Discussion*

Begin with your own responses to the realistic portrayal of the battle at the end of chapter 12. The starting point is not what you think you *should* feel but what you actually feel. Then ponder how your feelings in the matter are altered or reinforced by an awareness of the romance genre and the statements by Lewis and others about the value of realistic portrayals of evil and violence in literature, including children's literature.

Here is Lewis's reply to people who wish to protect a child against "the knowledge that he is born into a world of death, violence, wounds, adventure, heroism and cowardice, good and evil": Such shielding "would indeed ... give children a false impression and feed them on escapism in the bad sense. ... Since it is so likely that they will meet cruel enemies, let them at least have heard of brave knights and heroic courage. Otherwise you are making their destiny not brighter but darker. ... I side impenitently with the human race against the modern reformer. Let there be wicked kings and beheadings, battles and dungeons, giants and dragons, and let villains be soundly killed at the end of the book. Nothing will persuade me that this causes an ordinary child any kind or degree of fear beyond what it wants, and needs, to feel. For, of course, it wants to be a little frightened."

C. S. LEWIS, "ON THREE WAYS OF WRITING FOR CHILDREN"

13
Deep Magic from the Dawn of Time
The Uses of Magic

Literary magic is a much misunderstood subject on which we need to exercise some care and patience. A good starting point is to notice that the author himself, by virtue of the placement of these chapters, signals a connection between his use of magic and the deepest Christian roots of his story, dealing with the atonement of Christ. This already hints that C. S. Lewis intends magic to serve as a metaphor or symbol of spiritual meanings.

Second, the magic in the Narnian books is first of all a literary convention, not an occult phenomenon. As we have had occasion to note, one of the amazing aspects of *The Lion, the Witch and the Wardrobe* is the number of literary genres that converge in it. In virtually all of these genres, magic is present as part of the supernatural world of the story. This is true of the fairy story, myth and romance. Magic is common (though not essential to the genre) in fantasy literature, and readers of children's literature have a natural liking for touches of magic as well.

In the fairy tale, myth and romance, magic is not presented as something that exists literally in our own world but is rather a form the supernatural takes in the imagined "other" world of the story. Magic is a symbol or metaphor— something that *stands for* or *pictures* supernatural power, good and evil, in the universe. Ursula Le Guin speaks of the unrealistic aspects of fantasy as "metaphors of the human condition," and it is helpful to include magic among the elements of fantasy. No literal application to our world is intended.

*"We who hobnob with hobbits and tell tall tales about little green men
are quite used to being dismissed as mere entertainers,
or sternly disapproved of as escapists. . . . Realism is perhaps the least adequate
means of understanding or portraying the incredible realities of our existence.
A scientist who creates a monster in his laboratory . . .
a wizard unable to cast a spell: . . . all these may be precise and
profound metaphors of the human condition."*

URSULA LE GUIN, NATIONAL BOOK AWARD ACCEPTANCE SPEECH

MAGIC IN THE NARNIAN CHRONICLES AND THE HARRY POTTER BOOKS

With the rise of the Harry Potter phenomenon, a number of conservative Christian readers have begun to question the use of magic in children's stories, including the fiction of both J. R. R. Tolkien and C. S. Lewis. It is not our purpose here to give a definitive answer to the concerns raised by some about J. K. Rowling's Potter books (indeed the two of us have differing understandings of these books). However, it is important that readers understand how to distinguish between the literary uses of magic in Lewis (and similarly in Tolkien) and the wizardry of the Harry Potter books.

In the Narnian stories, Lewis makes use of only as much magic as is required by his chosen genres, given that magic is a required element in the literary world of the fairy tale, romance and myth. Further, Lewis's use of magic is actually an affirmation of the Christian worldview in which the supernatural is accepted as real. In this regard, note that magical interventions in the world of Faërie can be the equivalent of divine intervention or the miraculous in our own world.

In the Harry Potter books, magic is the central focus and draws attention to itself. Even here, some readers (not all) experience these stories primarily as classic school stories in which interactions among schoolmates and teachers are the key elements. For these readers, the basic story lines could be successfully lifted out of the imagined world and placed into another locale devoid of magic. The same cannot be said of the Narnian books, because in them magic affirms the transcendent power of Aslan and the reality of an unseen spiritual world.

Further, there are certain differences in the handling of magic within the stories. In the Narnian books, magic exists primarily in a fantasy world removed from our own world. The principal exception to this generalization is the magical entry from *our* world into Narnia that occurs in each of the seven books. Additionally, in *The Magician's Nephew* Uncle Andrew is a practicing, though inept, magician *living in London,* who fashions magic rings using dust from the lost island of Atlantis. In the Harry Potter books, the practice of magic is located in our own world, not another realm separate from our existence.

Second, magical events in *The Lion, the Witch and the Wardrobe* primarily happen by the power of supernatural agents, preserving a sense that they are manifestations of the power of supernatural beings. In Harry Potter, magic is usually the result of human spell casting, divination and occult practices. Lewis himself sheds light on this important distinction in the opening chapter of *The Silver Chair,* where Eustace and Jill are trying to escape from the bullies at their horrid school by finding a way into Narnia. As they discuss how they might somehow make this happen, Jill offers the suggestion that they draw a circle on the ground and recite charms—in other words, perform a classic incantation or spell that by its power will cause something else to occur. Eustace, who has already been in Narnia and been positively altered by meeting Aslan, is quick to refute this idea. He explains, "I believe that was the sort of thing I was thinking of, though I never did it. But now that it comes to the point, I've an idea that all those circles and things are rather rot. I don't think he'd like them. It would look *as if we thought we could make him do things.* But really, *we can only ask him*" (emphasis ours).

Here Lewis himself states what magic in Narnia truly entails: the children are not generally permitted to engage in magic but instead are invited to call on Aslan for his help (naturally, Christian readers will understand this as an invitation to engage in prayer in time of need). There is no doubt that in Lewis's Narnian stories, attempts to control circumstances through divination or spells are almost always wrong. There are occasional exceptions to this rule, as in Lucy's reading of the spell to make hidden things visible in the magician's book in *The Voyage of the "Dawn Treader."* In this instance, however, Lucy is not seeking her own interests but is performing a brave deed to help others.

To aid the reader in understanding this important distinction in purpose, Lewis labels other attempts at magic as black sorcery (for example, note the attempt by the wicked dwarf Nikabrik in *Prince Caspian* to conjure up some fearful malevolence; there is no doubt that his purpose is evil and that his action is resoundingly rejected by those who follow Aslan).

These distinctions allow us to understand the magic in the Narnian books as a purely literary device used primarily to express a transcendent Christian worldview. In the Harry Potter books, magic goes beyond the sparing use that such literary genres require, and it is not used to embody metaphorically the Christian supernatural (though many critics do emphasize the strong distinction that Rowling makes between good magic and that practiced by evil forces, and also that in Rowling's stories evil powers are ultimately defeated by the superior power of love, not simply by stronger magical powers).

> ### ⟨ *For Reflection or Discussion*
> Before looking at chapter 13, it could be profitable simply to take stock of how you have assimilated the magic of *The Lion, the Witch and the Wardrobe*. If you are also a reader of J. K. Rowling, reflect similarly on your experiences with the Harry Potter books.

PLOT DEVELOPMENTS IN CHAPTER 13

"Now we must get back to Edmund" (*LWW,* ch. 13, p. 134), the chapter begins. The Witch's entourage, which has been traveling interminably through the forest, halts in a dark valley. The Wolf returns from a scouting foray to announce that "they are all at the Stone Table, with Him." The Witch commands that "all our people" meet at the Stone Table, whereupon Edmund is bound to a tree. "Prepare the victim," the Witch commands (*LWW,* ch. 13, p. 136).

Then suddenly a conflict breaks out, freeing Edmund, who is eventually carried by the rescuing friendly forces (Aslan's) to the Stone Table. The next morning Edmund is reunited with his siblings after a private conversation with Aslan (significantly, the storyteller refuses to relay what is said during this long talk).

"A messenger from the enemy" (*LWW,* ch. 13, p. 139) is said to crave audience with Aslan. During negotiations between Aslan and the White Witch, the Witch appeals to "the Deep Magic" (*LWW,* ch. 13, p. 141). The latter includes the rule that every traitor legally belongs to the Witch and that unless the Witch has blood, Narnia will perish. After the parley, Aslan announces that the Witch has renounced her claim on Edmund's blood.

The sheer quantity of activity in the chapter is breathtaking, and as we read, we have the impression of listening to a code language referring to matters of which we have only a dim understanding. At a plot level, we have a sense that the conflict between Aslan and the White Witch is moving toward a climactic showdown. Mysterious foreshadowings of future action also leave us wondering exactly *how* the plot will be resolved. Finally, the biblical allusions and theological overtones are more pronounced than they have been thus far, though this thread will become much more explicit in the next two chapters.

The basic narrative framework of plot conflict will work its usual magic in making things fall into place. In contrast to the good animals and half-people that clustered around Aslan in the preceding chapter, the list of beasts that constitute the Witch's army is decidedly sinister: giants, werewolves, Ghouls, Boggles, Ogres, Minotaurs, Cruels, Hags, Specters and people of the Toadstools. Here is the demonic half of the literary imagination, which tends to give us good and bad manifestations of the same phenomena. Another main aspect of the ongoing plot conflict is the series of encounters between the White Witch and Aslan in the second half of the chapter.

Foreshadowing supplies a lot of voltage to developments of the plot in chapter 13. We do not yet know the significance of the Stone Table, but we sense that some climactic event will happen there. Aslan tells Mr. Beaver that "all names will soon be restored to their proper owners" (*LWW,* ch. 13, p. 140), leaving us to wonder what this means. Furthermore, at the end of the chapter, even though it is announced that Edmund will escape execution, the final action of the Lion's roar leaves us hanging as we wonder exactly how the rescue will be effected.

Third, adding to the elements of conflict and foreshadowing, the storytelling strategy of withholding information to generate mystery is used to powerful effect. For example, we infer that a battle has preceded Edmund's rescue from the tree to which he was bound, but we are given no details. And we naturally wonder what Aslan has said to Edmund in "a conversation which Edmund never forgot" (*LWW,* ch. 13, p. 139), but the narrator chooses reticence rather than disclosure.

⟨⟩ *For Reflection or Discussion*

Our analysis has given only a few illustrations of Lewis's techniques in chapter 13. Find other examples in these three areas (and others that occur to you):

- the details by which the conflict between good and evil is worked out
- foreshadowings of important actions that will follow
- examples of mystery and surprising omission of explanation (for example, *why* do you think Lewis chose not to include the details of the conversation between Aslan and Edmund?)

DECIPHERING THE "DEEP MAGIC" OF CHAPTER 13

The mention of "deep magic" in the title of the chapter signals a new religious seriousness in the story. There have been numerous signposts of this thematic development. One is the early mention of the four thrones in Cair Paravel: the after-dinner conversation at the Beavers' house (chapter 8) about a prophecy that when two Sons of Adam and two Daughters of Eve sit on these four thrones, the end of the White Witch will come.

Other references in chapter 13 add to our growing awareness of spiritual and theological overtones in the action. The battle between animals and half-humans seems to be more than a military battle in the romance mode. A guilty victim carried to a mysterious Stone Table hints at a scene of sacrificial expiation. Edmund's restoration to his siblings after Aslan tells them that "there is no need to talk to him about what is past" (*LWW*, ch. 13, p. 139) surely gestures toward a drama of forgiveness (even though that word is not used). Of similar import are the statement that "every traitor" is the Witch's "lawful prey" (*LWW*, ch. 13, p. 142) and references to a law that says Narnia will fall unless the Witch has blood as the penalty for treason. Overshadowing all of these are references to a "Deep Magic" that is governing the action at this point in the story.

14
The Triumph of the Witch
Parallels to the Passion Story

There can be no doubt that the Bible functions as a subtext for *The Lion, the Witch and the Wardrobe*—an understructure on which C. S. Lewis constructed *some* (but not all) of his story. But there is a right way and a wrong way to go about applying this principle.

A story needs to be allowed to set its own agenda. Any biblical element that we see in *The Lion, the Witch and the Wardrobe* needs to have some warrant in the text—some signal that the author intended us to bring the Bible into interpretive play. This contrasts with forcing the book onto a procrustean bed in which we see how many biblical echoes we can find in every part of the story.

Lewis himself asserted this principle: "A work of (whatever) art can be either 'received' or 'used.' When we 'receive' it we exert our senses and imagination and various other powers *according to a pattern invented by the artist*. When we 'use' it we treat it as assistance for our own activities." In other words, the story must be allowed to set its own agenda of topics and concerns. Applying this principle to *The Lion, the Witch and the Wardrobe*, we must be ready to see Christian meanings and biblical allusions in it where they exist, but not elsewhere.

If we follow the contours of the story as Lewis told it, it is obvious that the religious and biblical references cluster in the last five chapters. Until that point, the story is governed by the narrative dynamics of the fairy story and romance. Attempts to list Bible verses for every chapter of the book are word-association exercises, not insights into the story as Lewis told it. The arbitrary nature of the exercise is apparent when we stop to consider that we could do the same thing while reading the daily newspaper. Furthermore, searching for

---

The Metanarrative and Narnia

Lewis followed the model of the metanarrative when composing The Lion, the Witch and the Wardrobe. *The immediate events the children experience in Narnia are repeatedly placed against the backdrop of a bigger story (the metanarrative) involving Aslan's ongoing struggle with the White Witch, as well as references to the larger history of Narnia which precedes this immediate story. Even though we are made aware of this historical context, we do not as yet know much about it. If you have already read the other Narnian stories, you know that one of them,* The Magician's Nephew, *fills in pieces of this early history. There is debate among Lewis scholars as to whether the books should be read in the order of publication or according to the chronology of the metanarrative. For more on the proper reading order of the seven Narnian books, see the appendix to this volume.*

---

omnipresent biblical echoes results in moralizing rather than literary insight.

While biblical allusions do not abound equally in every part of *The Lion, the Witch and the Wardrobe,* there are ways in which the Bible can be seen as a presence all the way through. This has to do with overall narrative structure rather than specific references or parallels, and it concerns the Bible as a model and influence for how Lewis handled his material, not as a source of allusions.

Central to Lewis's enterprise in *The Lion, the Witch and the Wardrobe* is the theme of the two worlds. This refers to the premise that reality exists on two levels—the visible world in which we live and an unseen supernatural realm that is no less real. The invisible world interpenetrates our world and influences what happens in it. From beginning to end, the Bible exhibits a similar pattern of events happening on two levels—the earthly and the supernatural or otherworldly. While one cannot prove that Lewis was following the Bible as a literary model in this regard, it is a fair assumption, and in any case, the biblical model is a useful framework to have in our mind as we read.

Second, the Bible possesses what literary scholars call a metanarrative—a "big story" of which the individual stories and poems are individual "chapters." The big story is a story of cosmic, universal conflict between spiritual good and spiritual evil. The structure of the story is the shape of a U, and it has four main phases: God's creation of a perfect world, the loss of that world through the fall from innocence, fallen human history, and a final defeat of evil and restoration of the good. Within this history, the story of God's unfolding plan to redeem fallen creatures provides another metanarrative. Key points include God's dealings with a covenant people, his promises to send a savior, the coming of Christ as the atonement for human sins, and the participation of believers in this drama of forgiveness and salvation. As we read the Bible, the immediate foreground of its stories and poems keeps opening up into this larger story, of which we are nearly always aware.

ᐤ For Reflection or Discussion

You may wish to page through the book to locate passages that use the Bible's method of placing individual details into larger contexts, including the following:

- earthly experience set into relation to an "other," supernatural world (the theme of the two worlds)
- "windows" from the immediate action into a backdrop of the larger history of Narnia, with its story of cosmic battle between good and evil and of Aslan's redemptive life and resurrection as the decisive events in this great struggle

THE PASSION STORY DISPLACED INTO NARNIA

In addition to the large-scale presence of the Bible as a subtext as already noted, there are chapters late in the book where biblical parallels and allusions abound. Here the cautions stated above need not deter us. In fact, in chapter 14, the parallels to the story of Christ's suffering and crucifixion as narrated in the Gospels are so obvious that even Lewis's attempts to force a wedge between *The Lion, the Witch and the Wardrobe* and allegory begin to break down. We can take Lewis's word for it that he did not set out to see how many details of the passion story he could embody in his fantasy story. But we must equally remember that even though Lewis felt a need to assert that "at first there wasn't even anything Christian" about his fantasy pictures,

---

Past Watchful Dragons

It is a literary truism that one of the functions of literature is to defamiliarize experience—to transmute what has become dulled by familiarity into something new, with the result that we take note of it and are moved by it. Here is how English poet Samuel Taylor Coleridge expressed this idea: literature "rescues the most admitted truths from the impotence caused by the very circumstance of their universal admission. Truths . . . are too often considered as so true, that they lose all the life and efficiency of truth." Literature has the power to lead us to experience such truths "with a new feeling." Compare Coleridge's statement to Lewis's declaration of intent in terms of the Christian aspects of the Narnian stories: "I thought I saw how stories of this kind could steal past a certain inhibition which had paralysed much of my own religion in childhood. Why did one find it so hard to feel as one was told one ought to feel about God or about the sufferings of Christ? I thought the chief reason was that one was told one ought to. An obligation to feel can freeze feelings. . . . But supposing that by casting all these things into an imaginary world, stripping them of their stained-glass and Sunday School associations, one could make them for the first time appear in their real potency? Could one not thus steal past those watchful dragons? I thought one could."

he went on to say "that element pushed itself in of its own accord." In other words, the Christian meaning of the story is present because it existed already in the very fabric of Lewis's being—along the lines that "the only moral that is of any value is that which arises inevitably from the whole cast of an author's mind"—rather than being something that Lewis arbitrarily attempted to paste into the story.

It will be best for you to explore the parallels between the passion story in the Gospels and chapter 14 of *The Lion, the Witch and the Wardrobe* in ways that are most meaningful to you. To prime the pump, here are some key events and moments that will loom large in the exercise:

- a journey of Aslan and his followers to a place of execution, with Aslan giving his followers instructions for a coming battle as they travel
- an affecting and somber evening meal
- two sleepless followers (Lucy and Susan) trailing Aslan to the place of execution
- Aslan's announcement that is he sad and lonely
- the execution of Aslan amid jeering from demonically inspired tormenters
- unspeakable sadness as Aslan's death occurs

෴ *For Reflection and Discussion*

Here are avenues toward understanding the biblical aspects of Lewis' passion story:

- If you are so inclined, locate the specific biblical passages to which the details in chapter 14 allude.
- Notice nuances beyond the broad outline provided above that show links between the story that Lewis created and the passion story in the Gospels.
- This is a very moving story. Articulate the feelings that are elicited in you at various stages of the action.

15

Deeper Magic from
Before the Dawn of Time
The Genre of Fairy Tale

Aslan's death, narrated in chapter 14, marks the low point in the U-shaped plot of *The Lion, the Witch and the Wardrobe*. Chapter 15 is the turn-around, the point from which the story will rise to a happy ending. If chapter 14 is the passion story in the book, chapter 15 is the resurrection story. We should note, though, that there are fewer echoes from the Gospels in this chapter than in the preceding one.

The actual details in the text belong to a broad category known as the re-birth archetype. A literary critic has called this "the archetype of archetypes," in token of the frequency with which a turnaround from tragedy to the happy ending of comedy appears near the end of a story. Perhaps the desig-nation "archetype of archetypes" also tacitly acknowledges that the longing for rebirth is the most profound longing God has placed within the human psyche. Common forms in which the rebirth archetype is expressed in liter-ature including the following:

- resurrection of a dead being back to life
- imagery drawn from the spring season
- sunrise, or more generally passage from darkness to light
- physical transformation of a creature, either from death to life or from weakness to increasing strength

The mood that these archetypes evokes is relief and celebration. J. R. R. Tolkien popularized the concept of "Eucatastrophe" in fairy stories—the "good catastrophe" in which seeming defeat is transformed into victory. The accompanying mood, said Tolkien, is "Joy, Joy beyond the walls of the world, poignant as grief."

"It is the mark of a good fairy-story, of the higher or more complete kind, that however . . . terrible the adventures, it can give to child or man that hears it, when the 'turn' comes, a catch of the breath, a beat and lifting of the heart, near to (or indeed accompanied by) tears."

J. R. R. TOLKIEN, "ON FAIRY-STORIES"

℮ *For Reflection or Discussion*

A great deal of this rebirth story will fall into place if you apply what has been said above about the archetypal nature of the action in chapter 15:

- Some of the details that Lewis chose to include are so strongly parallel to events in the resurrection story in the Gospels that they can accurately be called *allusions*. Identifying them is crucial to an understanding of what is happening in this chapter.
- As the rebirth motif has been called "the archetype of archetypes," take stock of your literary memory to recall where you have encountered this archetype in the Bible and in your literary sojourns.
- Now look for specific rebirth images and motifs that Lewis incorporated into chapter 15.

THE GENRE OF THE FAIRY TALE

We have made references to the fairy tale genre throughout our discussion, and now it is time to look more formally at *The Lion, the Witch and the Wardrobe* as a fairy story. It may seem inappropriate to broach the subject as we reach the point in the story where we contemplate the resurrection of Jesus from the tomb and his appearance to the women and the Emmaus Road disciples on Easter Day. But chapter 15 almost requires to be approached in terms of fairy tale motifs. Just think about it: the equivalent in chapter 15 of the stone rolled away from the tomb is the spectacle of friendly mice gnawing through the cords that had bound Aslan the lion.

Before we think about the specific fairy tale motifs that Lewis employs in his resurrection story, it will be good to get a grip on the fairy story as a genre. Fairy tales are a primitive genre, meaning that they have been around from the beginnings of recorded history. The fairy tale is a simple form that can rightly be called a form of folk literature, appealing to children as well as adults and to people with simple literary abilities as well as the literati of society. Reflecting upon the universal appeal of fairy tales, Frederick Buechner writes, "there has never been an age that has not produced fairy tales."

"There has never been an age that has not produced fairy tales.
It doesn't seem to matter what is going on at the time. . . . No matter what's up politically,
economically, religiously, artistically, people always seem to go on telling these stories,
many of them stories that have been around for so long that it is as impossible to be sure
when they first started as it is to be sure when if ever they will finally end."
FREDERICK BUECHNER, *TELLING THE TRUTH*

Fairy stories present a simplified world in which obvious good is in conflict with obvious evil. Characters are correspondingly polarized, being either good or bad. Because virtually all of the experts on fairy stories agree that they awaken longing for an ideal world, one might be misled into thinking they are a form of wish-fulfillment literature. The opposite is true: the world of fairy tales is a dark world of danger and threatening evil, and at many points fairy stories intersect with the genre of horror story.

Part of the horror is that disguises are prevalent in fairy stories. Bad characters are disguised as good agents. Of course good characters are also disguised, and their true identities are eventually revealed, but until the revelation they are denied the freedom to do what good characters do.

Magical or marvelous events are a prime characteristic of fairy stories, which is a way of saying that they belong to the broader category of fantasy literature. Buechner notes that in fairy stories "beasts talk and flowers come alive, . . . and nothing is apt to be what it seems."

While all of the foregoing traits relate to the narrative qualities of fairy tales, everyone who has thought deeply about the genre agrees that there is something deeper going on in these stories—a longing that comes through the particulars. Here is how Lewis, Tolkien and Buechner identify this deeper "something" that emerges from fairy stories:

- Popular children's stories and fairy stories both "arouse, and imaginatively satisfy, wishes," Lewis writes. "We long to go through the looking glass, to reach fairy land. We also long to be the immensely popular and successful schoolboy or schoolgirl. . . . But the two longings are very different. . . . A child does not long for fairy land as a boy longs to be the hero of [his class]. . . . Fairy land arouses a longing for he knows not what. It stirs and troubles him (to his life-long enrichment) with the dim sense of something beyond his reach and, far from dulling or emptying the actual world, gives it a new dimension of depth."

- In his classic essay "On Fairy-Stories," Tolkien writes, "Fairy-stories were plainly not primarily concerned with possibility, but with desirability. If they awakened *desire,* satisfying it while often whetting it unbearably, they succeeded. . . . Fairy-stories offer also, in a peculiar degree or mode, these things: Fantasy, Recovery, Escape, Consolation."

- Frederick Buechner, in his essay "The Gospel as Fairy Tale," writes, "Beneath the specific events and adventures they describe, what gives them their real power and meaning is the world they evoke. . . . For all its confusion and wildness, it is a world where the battle goes ultimately to the good. . . . It is perhaps this aspect of the fairy tale that gives it its greatest power over us."

To apply this in a general way to the Narnian books, we can do no better than to heed the advice that Lewis gave regarding Edmund Spenser's

Faerie Queene, which has been subjected to as much intellectual analysis as any work in English literature. While not denying that allegorical and intellectual meanings are present in the work, Lewis insisted in numerous places on the principle that "it is of course much more than a fairy-tale, but unless we can enjoy it as a fairy-tale first of all, we shall not really care for it."

On Spenser's Faerie Queene: "Its primary appeal is to the most naïve and innocent tastes. . . . It demands of us a child's love of marvels and dread of bogies, a boy's thirst for adventures. . . . If you have lost or cannot re-arouse these attitudes, all the commentaries, all your scholarship . . . will not avail.
The poem is a great palace, but the door into it is so low that you must stoop to go in."
C. S. LEWIS, *STUDIES IN MEDIEVAL AND RENAISSANCE LITERATURE*

ᏊᎦ *For Reflection or Discussion*

Before we turn to chapter 15 as a fairy tale, you might wish to take stock of the story as a whole, noting features that show its fairy tale identity. What do you think Lewis meant when he said that he "wrote fairy tales because the Fairy Tale seemed the ideal Form for the stuff I had to say"?

FAIRY TALE MOTIFS OF CHAPTER 15

It is time to take a second look at chapter 15. Fairy tales, being a primitive form and an example of the folk imagination, naturally rely heavily on archetypes for their basic substance. Yet it would be wrong to assume that the archetypes we noted earlier are distinctive to the fairy tale identity of chapter 15.

The title speaks of "deeper magic," so we can start with the element of the marvelous as part of the fairy-story aspect of this chapter. The concept of "deeper magic" is articulated by Aslan himself halfway through, and it is given a theological significance, inasmuch as Aslan relates it to the destruction of "Death itself," based on the actions of "a willing victim who had committed no treachery [being] killed in a traitor's stead" (*LWW*, ch. 15, p. 163). But there are numerous examples of less profound marvels, many of them having to do with the actions of friendly animals (including Aslan as lion).

Part of the appeal of fairy stories like chapter 15 is the presence of stock moments or conventions of the form. Children as characters, for example, are part of the appeal, as in this chapter the wonderful events happen to Lucy and Susan, not to adults. The playfulness with which Aslan and the girls interact in the second half of the chapter is an expression of childhood, as even Aslan becomes childlike in his joyful and boisterous response. Other stock ingredients of the fairy tale include flying through space and looking at a distant castle that appears like "a little toy castle."

ᏊᏊ *For Reflection or Discussion*

At least three avenues exist to experiencing and relishing the fairy tale nature of chapter 15:

- Comb the chapter for places where the fairy tale convention of the marvelous or magical embodies the deeper meanings of the resurrection story.
- As Buechner notes, fairy stories of all places and times "seem to have certain features in common." Try to recall parallels to chapter 15 from your other literary travels through fairyland.
- The main narrative business of chapter 15 is joyous celebration. Scrutinize the fairy tale qualities of the chapter to see how they are particularly effective in achieving the mood of festive celebration.

16

What Happened About the Statues
The Role of Myth

Just before chapter 16 starts, Aslan has arrived at the home of the White Witch and deposited Lucy and Susan "tumbling off his back in the middle of a wide stone courtyard full of statues" (*LWW,* ch. 15, p. 166). We remember what the statues mean—living creatures transformed by the Witch into frozen stone—but we are shocked by how *many* there are. The main action of chapter 16 is Aslan's returning the statues to their living forms. It is impossible to enter into the spirit of the chapter without evoking the literary form known as myth.

The Lion, the Witch and the Wardrobe represents a convergence of several interrelated genres, including fairy story, myth, fantasy and romance. All four of these employ the marvelous, as literary scholars term it (supernatural characters, settings and events that do not exist in visible form in our own world). This common feature should not, however, be allowed to obscure the differences that exist among these genres.

We have not said much about myth in connection with *The Lion, the Witch and the Wardrobe,* and in fact the story is less akin to myth than it is to the other three genres that employ the marvelous. Yet some moments in the story strike the authentic mythical note, including this chapter in which statues come to life. Here are some starting descriptors that enable us to label a story as belonging to myth:

- Some of the characters are divine—gods, goddesses and perhaps demons, not simply fantastic creatures like talking animals.
- Some of the events that are narrated are likewise supernatural.

Norse Mythology

From an early age, C. S. Lewis was captivated by the stories and legends of what he called "Northernness." This love of Norse mythology first originated when, as a young boy, he read a few lines from Longfellow's version of Esaias Tegner's Drapa about the death of Balder the Beautiful. Lewis later recalled that though he knew nothing of Balder at the time, he was "instantly . . . uplifted into huge regions of northern sky, I desired with almost sickening intensity something never to be described (except that it is cold, spacious, severe, pale, and remote)." In reading Norse myths, Lewis found himself drawn to a sense of wildness, to the "twilight of a Northern summer," to something remote and severe in its beauty, but also to something unattainable, an inconsolable longing, which he named Joy. It is helpful for readers of The Lion, the Witch and the Wardrobe to be aware of Lewis's great love for myth and the impact that it had on his spiritual and literary development.

- The setting for the action is a spiritual world that transcends the earthly realm.
- Yet it is always visible, literal and explicit. In a myth we do not experience a merely psychological "desert" of the spirit, for example; instead we encounter a *real desert*, a land of dry desolation where the sun beats down relentlessly on parched sand dunes.
- Ancient myths were believed to be expressions of religious truth by the cultures that produced or perpetuated them.
- Thus rather than communicating "facts" or history, myths convey "truth"—and even more significantly, what we would term *universal* truth.
- Being a primitive form of literature, myths are stories in which we can see archetypal patterns in their most simplified form.
- All great myths appeal *primarily* to the imagination rather than to the intellect.

It might be helpful to think of myth as representing certain tendencies that are also present in the other three related genres (fairy story, romance, fantasy) *to a greater degree.* For example, there are bigger-than-life creatures, but not gods, in fairy stories and fantasy. In fantasy, a character might use a magic potion to subdue another person, but the circumstance of statues coming to life represents a higher degree of transcending ordinary life.

Myth

Lewis presented his own interpretation of myth in a chapter in An Experiment in Criticism. *Here are the traits that he ascribed to myth:*

- *Mythical stories are so striking in themselves that their power over the human psyche is inherent in the stories, quite apart from the literary skill, or lack of it, with which a given storyteller has told the story.*
- *Mythical stories "have a very simple narrative shape—a satisfactory and inevitable shape, like a good vase or a tulip."*
- *"Even at a first hearing [a mythic tale] is felt to be inevitable."*
- *The characters in a mythical story do not primarily appeal to us as fellow human beings; rather, "they are like shapes moving in another world."*
- *Myth is a type of fantasy story that "deals with impossibles and preternaturals"—in other words, it transcends our natural world and moves into the realm of the "supernatural."*
- *The experiences portrayed "may be sad or joyful" but are "always grave" and weighty. Myth cannot be comic.*
- *"The experience is not only grave but awe-inspiring. We feel it to be numinous." In myth, there is a sense of awe and of the wholly transcendent "other."*

It has long been recognized that myth is a meeting ground between literature and religion, partly because ancient myths were part of the religious system of the cultures producing and perpetuating them and partly because the supernaturalism of myth makes it akin to religion. Whether the mythic impulse is friend or foe to Christianity continues to be debated, and Lewis made significant contributions to this discussion. In brief, he believed that myths are glimmers of truth that God has sent to pagan people to aid their awareness of the transcendent realities that surround them. To Lewis, "the resemblance between these myths and the Christian truth is no more accidental than the resemblance between the sun and the sun's reflection in a pond, or that between a historical fact and the somewhat garbled version of it which lives in popular report." Indeed, in his own life, myth helped him come to a point where he was able to acknowledge God's saving presence in the world.

For Reflection or Discussion

Before turning to the mythical aspects of chapter 16, you might wish to take stock of the story as a whole, asking the following questions among other potential ones:

- What parts of *The Lion, the Witch and the Wardrobe* strike you as moving beyond fantasy into the realm of myth? What leads you to see these elements as mythic?

- How do the parts of the story that you consider mythical differ from the other parts, in terms of both narrative qualities and thematic content?

MYTHIC ACTION IN CHAPTER 16

As we begin our look at chapter 16, let's heed Lewis's reminder that our first task is to enjoy "the central, obvious appeal" of the story—the surface details. The journey of Aslan and the two girls through a gallery of statues that come to life is an adventure story of the first order. Before we resort to religious musings, we need to relive the excitement of the external action, as "the courtyard looked no longer like a museum; it looked more like a zoo." The sheer variety of creatures named in the chapter is a creative tour de force. Humor and lightheartedness reenter the story. The adventure even includes a battle at the end of the chapter.

In addition to the surface adventure, we can relish the archetypal richness of the scene, searching our literary memory for other versions of the motif of transformation of people or animals into statues or other inanimate objects. In Homer's *Odyssey,* the god Poseidon gets even with the people who transported Odysseus to his homeland by turning their ship into stone as it comes sailing back into the harbor. The biblical story of the transformation of Lot's wife into a pillar of salt belongs to the same archetype. The most famous transformation scene in English literature is the last scene of Shakespeare's play *The Winter's Tale,* in which a wife in the form of a statue comes to life and is restored to her husband. The greatest repository of mythical stories of transformation is the Roman poet Ovid's *Metamorphoses.*

The idea of transformation is archetypal because it expresses a principle of life and of spiritual reality. In its own way, chapter 16 is a rebirth story as well as a rescue story. Spiritual overtones naturally enter our awareness as we read, especially when Aslan defeats the White Witch in single combat in the battle at the end of the chapter. Biblical passages that speak of hearts of stone being replaced by hearts of flesh (Ezekiel 11:19; 36:26) may naturally come to our mind.

Ꮭ *For Reflection or Discussion*

All of the foregoing frameworks provide lenses by which to make sense of the elements Lewis includes in this chapter—adventure, rebirth and other archetypes, and the mythic and spiritual significance of what is happening. Having looked at these aspects individually, you may want to watch for how the various threads are integrated, so that, for example, an adventure is also an archetype that embodies some spiritual significance.

17

The Hunting of the White Stag
The Happy Ending as Narrative Pattern and Spiritual Reality

In the earlier discussion of the plot structure of *The Lion, the Witch and the Wardrobe,* we mentioned the architectonic shapeliness of the story's overall plot. Here at the conclusion we can see even more clearly than before that the overall design of the plot is a U-shaped pattern, with descent into potential tragedy and then ascent to a happy ending. Storytellers from time immemorial have felt a strong pressure, either from within or from their readers and listeners, to make the action turn out happily. A good example of the pattern of the happy ending after terrible ordeal and tragedy is the last chapter of the Old Testament book of Job.

Before you probe the deeper meanings of the happy ending of *The Lion, the Witch and the Wardrobe,* it is important to absorb the literal details that make up this ending. From one point of view, these details are such a swirl of activity that the story borders on a festive chaos here. So strong is the romance pressure for battlefield action that Lewis can't resist one more battle scene at the outset of the chapter, in which Lucy becomes a veritable Florence Nightingale tending to the wounded. There are multiple teas and a march to the castle at Cair Paravel, followed by coronations. And these are only the *beginning* of happy events.

> ### ᏸ *For Reflection or Discussion*
> The happy ending asks to be experienced and enjoyed before it is subjected to intellectual inquiry into deeper meanings. Compile an inven-

tory, then, of all the things that take place in the orchestra of this particular happy ending.

DEEPER MEANINGS OF THE HAPPY ENDING

The happy ending in a fairy tale like *The Lion, the Witch and the Wardrobe* is more than a narrative convention. It also embodies a principle of life and ultimately a reality of the Christian faith.

The person who has written definitively on the happy ending in fairy stories is J. R. R. Tolkien, in his classic essay "On Fairy-Stories." Tolkien begins by claiming that "the Consolation of the Happy Ending" is one of four qualities that fairy stories possess in a unique way, the other three being "Fantasy, Recovery, Escape." Regarding the happy ending, Tolkien says, "Almost I would venture to assert that all complete fairy-stories must have it." Convinced that the happy ending is the "highest function" of the fairy tale, Tolkien even coined the word *eucatastrophe* to name the phenomenon. His own definition is this: "the consolation of fairy-stories, the joy of the happy ending: or more correctly of the good catastrophe, the sudden joyous 'turn.'"

And what is the spiritual meaning of this happy ending? First, "it denies (in the face of much evidence, if you will) universal final defeat and in so far is *evangelium,* giving a fleeting glimpse of Joy, Joy beyond the walls of the world." Then, in his most daring assessment of all, Tolkien claims that "the Christian Story" of Christ's atoning death and resurrection "embraces all the essence of fairy-stories." It is important to understand that in making this statement Tolkien is not casting doubt on the historical reality of the Christian story; rather, he is declaring his deep faith in the joyful power and spiritual reality that is truly and completely fulfilled in the life of Christ.

Frederick Buechner has written in a similar vein that "good and evil meet and do battle in the fairy tale world much as they meet and do battle in our

"The Gospels contain a fairy-story. . . . They contain many marvels—
peculiarly artistic, beautiful, and moving. . . .
The Birth of Christ is the eucatastrophe of Man's history.
The Resurrection is the eucatastrophe of the story of the Incarnation.
The story begins and ends in joy. . . . This story is supreme; and it is true.
Art has been verified. . . . The Evangelium has not abrogated legends;
it has hallowed them, especially the 'happy ending.'"

J. R. R. TOLKIEN, "ON FAIRY-STORIES," IN *TOLKIEN READER*

world, but in fairy tales the good live happily ever after. That is the major difference." In his essay "The Gospel as Fairy Tale," Buechner notes that the life of Christ in the Gospels contains some of the same motifs as fairy stories, including "the final victory of light. That is the fairy tale of the Gospel with, of course, the one crucial difference from all other fairy tales, which is that the claim made for it is that it is true."

For Reflection or Discussion

- Your personal experience of the narrative phenomenon of the happy ending is a good starting point. How do happy endings affect you? When do they ring true?

- In what ways do you think that Tolkien's theory on the religious significance of the happy ending in fairy stories and parallels to the Christian gospel is true?

- Next you may want to read through chapter 17 again, looking for signposts that the flurry of fairy tale events is intended to open up into a spiritual reality beyond the surface of the story.

THE JOURNEY OUT OF NARNIA

The moments of transition between the fictional real world and the fantasy world of Narnia surely rank among our favorite parts of the Narnian stories. They allow Lewis to exercise his inventiveness in particularly pleasing ways. Early in *The Lion, the Witch and the Wardrobe* we experienced three successive passages from the country house where the children are staying into the land of Narnia. Here at the end of the book, Lewis needs to get the children back through the wardrobe.

> ### ⌢ *For Reflection or Discussion*
> Take another close look at how Lewis manages the journey out of Narnia and back into the real world. What surprises you? What strikes you as cleverly conceived and executed?

THE ENDING OF THE STORY

We noted at the outset of this exploration of *The Lion, the Witch and the Wardrobe* that the two most crucial tests of a storyteller are the story's beginning and end. Two things in particular are important about story endings.

First, consider how you would answer the question, how do we know when a story is finished? There is not necessarily just one right answer, but one answer is indisputable. A story is over when the main concerns that have been introduced into the story are resolved. But of course figuring this out requires some time and analysis. We need to determine the key issues that have been introduced into *The Lion, the Witch and the Wardrobe* along the way.

Before we mention a second important ingredient in story endings, here are a few famous endings for you to relish:

- "And they lived happily ever after." (the conventional ending of fairy stories and many children's stories)
- "Some natural tears they dropped, but wiped them soon;
  The world was all before them, where to choose

Departures Home

Here is how Lewis chose to fashion the moments of transition in his other six children's stories when his characters leave Narnia and return to their own "real world."

- Prince Caspian. *The four children (Peter, Susan, Edmund and Lucy) return to their own world through a "doorway" made out of three stakes of wood that Aslan orders constructed in a forest glade. Before walking through this doorway, Peter and Susan are alerted that they are now too old to remain in Narnia and will not be able to return in the future, but Lucy and Edmund are not so warned. After walking through the doorway, the children find themselves back at the same country railway station where this journey to Narnia began.*

- The Voyage of the "Dawn Treader." *Lucy and Edmund are told that this will be their last time in Narnia (while Eustace will return once again). Their return to England is by way of a door that Aslan creates for them high in the sky. Upon returning, they find themselves back in the guest bedroom in Eustace's Cambridge home.*

- The Silver Chair. *Aslan blows Eustace and Jill away from Narnia and back to the Mountain of Aslan (where their adventure first began); here they watch Aslan bring King Caspian back to life. Caspian is then given permission to return with Eustace and Jill to their world for a brief time to help them teach the bullies of their boarding school, Experiment House, a lesson. They return to their world through a gap in the school wall, which has been knocked down by Aslan's tremendous roar.*

- The Horse and His Boy. *Because all the action of this story takes place during the period when the four children (Peter, Susan, Edmund and Lucy) reign as kings and queens over the inhabitants of Narnia (in the final pages of* The Lion, the Witch and the Wardrobe), *there is no transition into or out of Narnia.*

- The Magician's Nephew. *Though the children used magic rings to enter Narnia, they need no magic to return home. Aslan first accompanies the children to the "Wood between the Worlds." Then, after simply looking up into his face, the children find themselves transported home by Aslan's mighty power.*

- The Last Battle. *In this final story of the Chronicles of Narnia, the seven friends of Narnia, children from the earlier stories, find themselves unexpectedly inside a stable in Narnia. Once there, they discover to their amazed delight that the stable's inside is much, much bigger than its outside—for they are no longer in Narnia. At long last, they have entered Aslan's own country ("further up and further in"), a great land that contains all they that they have ever loved, a land where the real Narnia and the real England exist side by side forever. There will be no more transitions. They are home at last.*

Their place of rest, and Providence their guide:

They hand in hand, with wand'ring steps and slow,

Through Eden took their solitary way." (John Milton, *Paradise Lost*)

- "I took her hand in mine, and we went out of the ruined place; and, as the morning mists had risen long ago when I first left the forge, so the evening mists were rising now, and in all the broad expanse of tranquil light they showed to me, I saw no shadow of another parting from her." (Charles Dickens, *Great Expectations*)

- "[What] calls upon us, by the grace of Grace [i.e., God]

  We will perform in measure, time, and place.

  So thanks to all at once and to each one,

  Whom we invite to see us crowned at Scone." (William Shakespeare, *Macbeth*)

All of these endings not only announce the end of the story but also paradoxically point forward to further action. In a sense they are both an ending and the hint of a beginning or continuation. Now consider the last paragraph of *The Lion, the Witch and the Wardrobe*: "And that is the very end of the adventures of the wardrobe. But if the Professor was right it was only the beginning of the adventures of Narnia" (*LWW*, ch. 17, p. 189). (The paragraph that precedes this one also points forward to future action.)

The capstone ending, narrated in the final volume of the Narnian stories, The Last Battle, is as follows:

- And as He spoke He no longer looked to them like a lion; but the things that began to happen after that were so great and beautiful that I cannot write them. And for us this is the end of all the stories, and we can most truly say that they all lived happily ever after. But for them it was only the beginning of the real story. All their life in this world and all their adventures in Narnia had only been the cover and the title page: now at last they were beginning Chapter One of the Great Story, which no one on earth has read: which goes on for ever: in which every chapter is better than the one before.

ᙅᐧᐧ *For Reflection or Discussion*

- Take time to codify your understanding of the main issues that were introduced into the story, and then ponder how they are resolved by the time we end the story.

- Is the ending of *The Lion, the Witch and the Wardrobe* a good or effective ending? Why or why not?

- Ever since the time of Aristotle, literary scholars have talked about catharsis (literally, "purging") as a quality of great literature. Literary catharsis is the state of emotional and mental calm or equilibrium that readers or viewers feel at the end of a story, after great issues and emotions have been raised and subdued. What elements bring you equilibrium at the end of *The Lion, the Witch and the Wardrobe?*

18

Retrospective
Putting It All Together

Ｔhe End. *Finis* (Latin word meaning "end, close, stop"). Storytellers sometimes use a formula like these to signal that the story is finished. But of course good stories are not finished simply because we have read the last sentence. They live on in our experience and memory. In fact, it is only after we have completed a story that certain features of it fall into final form.

Here are some avenues to putting it all together in regard to *The Lion, the Witch and the Wardrobe:*

- The impressionistic question is always a good starting point for reflection or discussion: What for you is most important in *The Lion, the Witch and the Wardrobe?* What do you like most about the story? What do you dislike?

- Literary critic Northrop Frye made an important observation about the difference between the actual reading of a story and our retrospective grasp of it. In brief, Frye said (and most readers' experiences will confirm its truthfulness) that whereas during the act of reading the sequential flow is what most absorbs our attention, afterward the sense of sequence is one of the most difficult things to recall. What we remember instead is individual bits and pieces and overall impressions. A good "taking stock" question therefore is, what general qualities and specific events or details stand out most in your mind as you look back? What did C. S. Lewis do best in *The Lion, the Witch and the Wardrobe?*

"In our direct experience of fiction we feel how central is the importance
of the steady progression of events that holds and guides our attention.
Yet afterwards, when we try to remember or think about what we have seen,
this sense of continuity is one of the most difficult things to recapture.
What stands out in our minds is a vivid characterization, a great speech or
striking image, a detached scene, bits and pieces of unusually convincing realization."

NORTHROP FRYE, *FABLES OF IDENTITY*

- A modern literary theorist titled one of his books *The Pleasures of the Text.* The title draws our attention to an important question that we should ask of books that we like: for you personally, what are the *pleasures* of reading *The Lion, the Witch and the Wardrobe?*
- Thomas Hardy said about stories that "a story must be exceptional enough to justify its telling." Storytellers are always on the lookout for good story material. What are the aspects of the story itself that make *The Lion, the Witch and the Wardrobe* a good story?

- In addition to what has traditionally been called the "matter" of a story (the content), the storyteller's skill has been a prime avenue toward analyzing and praising a story. Besides the interesting content of Lewis' story, what for you are the aspects of Lewis's skill as a storyteller and (potentially) stylist that make *The Lion, the Witch and the Wardrobe* the successful story that readers have found it to be?

- Of course there is the additional level of theme, worldview and profundity of human experience in a great story. It is true that storytellers are always on the lookout for good material on which they can exercise their creative skill, but they also gravitate toward stories in which (to use the formula of nineteenth-century French writer Charles Baudelaire) "the deep significance of life reveals itself." What aspects of *The Lion, the Witch and the Wardrobe* reveal the deep significance of life? What specific aspects of life are clarified or affirmed in the story?

IS *THE LION, THE WITCH AND THE WARDROBE* A CLASSIC?

Whether a given work is a classic is something readers need to answer for themselves. Here are some good definitions of what makes a story a classic. *You* be the judge of whether *The Lion, the Witch and the Wardrobe* meets one or more of these criteria. As you read the definitions, some adaptation will need to be made, given that *The Lion, the Witch and the Wardrobe* is a children's story that has its supreme stature within a certain subculture of our broader society.

- "[A masterpiece] modifies our very being and makes us feel . . . that we are not the same men and women we were when we began it" (Sheldon Sacks).

- "We speak of a book as a classic when it has gained a place for itself in our culture, and has consequently become a part of our educational experience" (Harry Levin).

- "[A great book] lays its images permanently on the mind [and] is entirely irreplaceable in the sense that no other book whatever comes anywhere near reminding you of it or being even a momentary substitute for it" (C. S. Lewis).

- "What we tend to require for something called a literary masterwork is a display of great craftsmanship [and] . . . striking originality. . . . Beyond this . . . the text must make a powerful emotional and intellectual impact, provide a rich reading experience, and leave behind . . . a new way to think about our lives. In the case of the greatest works, we return to them time and again in our minds, even if we do not reread them frequently" (Nina Baym).

A footnote to the question of whether and how *The Lion, the Witch and the Wardrobe* has the status of a classic is the way in which we describe it as a family classic. Among the reasons Philip Ryken gives for Lewis's popularity among American evangelicals is a phenomenon that he labels "fun for the whole family." (Ryken also recalls that as a child "I did not have a really satisfactory illness unless I had time to read all seven *Narnian Chronicles,* either in canonical or chronological order.")

ON THE REREADING OF STORIES

It is a rare reader who hears or reads the Narnian books only once. What Lewis said of Edmund Spenser's *Faerie Queene* is true of his own Narnian books: "It seldom loses those it has once gained. I never meet a man who says that he *used to* like the *Faerie Queene*." Lewis also made pretty clear his own views on the rereading of literary classics.

To begin, Lewis had a pejorative view of people who read good books only once. "The sure mark of an unliterary man," wrote Lewis, "is that he considers 'I've read it already' to be a conclusive argument against reading a work." Again, "There is hope for a man who has never read Malory or Boswell or *Tristram Shandy* or Shakespeare's *Sonnets:* but what can you do with a man who says he 'has read' them, meaning he has read them once, and thinks that this settles the matter?"

But what of people who reread books? Such rereading is first of all a comment on the needs and satisfactions that a reader finds in specific works. "If you find that the reader of popular romance—however uneducated a reader, however bad the romances—goes back to his old favourites again and again, then you have pretty good evidence that they are to him a sort of poetry." Further, the test of rereading is a comment on the quality of the book itself: "Those who read great works . . . will read the same work ten, twenty or thirty times during the course of their life."

Furthermore, great works of literature are inexhaustible in the sense that they keep meaning more and different things to the same reader as the reader's experiences of life change and deepen. Lewis hints at this when he writes, "I think my growth is just as apparent when I now read the fairy tales as when I read the novelists, for I now enjoy the fairy tales better than I did in childhood: being now able to put more in, of course I get more out."

Most readers who know the Narnian books first encountered them in their childhood, and many of these heard the stories read aloud before they read them. For such people, the idea of "rereading" the Narnian books includes a comparison of the child's (probably) oral first encounter and the adult's later encounters. Peter Schakel cites the case of a student who recalled her first encounters with the Narnian books as a child being read to. Among the insights that the student shared were these:

- The child listening to the stories does not control the pace of the reading.
- With no possibility of reading ahead, skipping pages or speed-reading to reach the end, the listener is forced to live in the present moment of the story as it is being presented by reader to listener. The result is a slower, more deliberative experience of the stories than reading ordinarily achieves.
- To the listening child, therefore, the action is unbearably suspenseful.
- The stories seemed much longer to the listening child than they do to the reading adult.
- Free from the need to read the words on the page, the child's imagination could seize upon the images, characters and events of the stories and experience them more directly and vividly.

One of the memories of this person's experience of hearing the stories for the first time was the suspense that the stories generated. While the first-time experience can never be completely duplicated, we should remember Lewis's point that in really great stories such first-time narrative qualities as suspense, surprise and curiosity about outcome live on even though (or perhaps because) readers know what plot twists are coming. Additionally, what counts as suspense on a first reading in subsequent readings often becomes dramatic irony (a situation in which readers have more information at their disposal than characters in the story do).

For Reflection or Discussion

- If you are a rereader of the Narnian books, it will doubtless prove interesting and informative to engage in some introspection about the issues just discussed. How do your first encounters with the books compare with later ones?
- If applicable, consider what remains constant and what changes between a child's experience of the Narnian stories and an adult's experience of them.
- If it is true, as psychological literary critics like Bruno Bettelheim and Simon Lesser claim, that what we see in books and even our selection of books for reading reflect our inner needs of the moment, what are the implications of this for your latest rereading of one of the Narnian tales?

Albert James Lewis (1863-1929), father of C. S. ("Jack") and Warren Lewis, 1925. Albert was a successful solicitor (lawyer) in the police courts of Belfast. He never remarried after his wife's death.

Florence ("Flora") Augusta Hamilton Lewis (1862-1908), mother of Jack and Warren Lewis, ca. 1897. Lewis's mother was the daughter of a Church of Ireland clergyman and a graduate of Queen's University, Belfast. She died at the young age of 46 from cancer, when Jack was not quite 10 years old.

C. S. Lewis as a young boy of about 3, posed in a professional studio portrait with a Father Christmas toy. When Lewis rechristened himself "Jack," he was about this age.

Albert and C. S. Lewis
Jack and his father in the garden of their Belfast family home, Little Lea, in July 1919. This photograph was taken by Warren Lewis while Jack was home on vacation from his studies at Oxford.

Lewis Family
This Lewis family portrait was taken on the steps of Little Lea, Belfast, northern Ireland in 1905. From l. to r., first row: Warren Lewis (age 10), C. S. "Jack" Lewis (age 7), Leonard Lewis (cousin), and Eileen Lewis (cousin). Second row: Agnes Young Lewis (aunt), maid, maid, Flora Hamilton Lewis (mother), and Albert Lewis (father) holding the dog Nero.

C. S. and Warren Lewis
This photograph of Jack and Warnie with their bicycles was taken outside Glenmachen, the Belfast home of their Ewart cousins, in August 1908—the month their mother died. Jack was almost 10. Warnie was just 13.

C. S. Lewis in the Little End Room, Little Lea

This photograph of C. S. Lewis (Jack) at age 21 was taken by his brother Warren in December 1919. By this time, Jack had completed his war service and was back at Oxford University as a student.

C. S. Lewis

This portrait of C. S. Lewis was taken after he had been wounded in World War I, and was home on leave, ca. 1919. Note his armband which is worn in remembrance of fallen comrades.

Lewis brothers and Mrs. Moore
Jack Lewis, his "adopted" mother Janie King Moore, and his brother, Warnie, outside the Kilns, in autumn 1930.

The Kilns
This photograph of the Kilns, Lewis's home outside Oxford, was taken by Warren Lewis in October 1930, shortly after they (Jack, Warnie and Mrs. Moore) purchased the house and its spacious eight acre grounds. Jack was to live at the Kilns more than thirty years, until his death in November 1963.

C. S. Lewis and his two stepsons, David (left) and Douglas Gresham, outside the Kilns
After the death of Joy in 1960, Lewis continued to care for his two stepsons (then aged 16 and 15).

Joy Davidman Gresham Lewis (1915-1960) (photographer: Chad Walsh)
A talented poet and writer, Joy Davidman was born in New York City to Jewish parents. After initially corresponding with C. S. Lewis about his books, she first met him in 1952. A friendship developed, and they eventually fell in love. They were married in a civil ceremony in 1956; followed by an Anglican one in 1957 at her hospital bedside after she was diagnosed with cancer. Their marriage was an unusually happy one, but sadly, Joy was to die at the young age of 45 after only three years of marriage.

C. S. Lewis
working at his desk in the Kilns, August 1960. This photograph was taken just a month after the death of his wife, Joy Davidman Lewis.

C. S. ("Jack") Lewis
in 1938. It is likely that this photograph was taken by his brother Warren while they were on one of their beloved walking tours of the countryside. In 1938, they spent four days walking through Wiltshire, England.

PART TWO

NARNIAN BACKGROUNDS

19

How the Narnian Books Came to Be

As with most creative enterprises, determining precisely how the Narnian stories came into being is slightly elusive; C. S. Lewis himself was uncertain exactly what precipitated his initial impulse to write a children's story. As he later explained, while still in the midst of writing his seven books: "I am not quite sure what made me, in a particular year of my life, feel that not only a fairy tale, but a fairy tale addressed to children, was exactly what I must write—or burst." He did, however, recall several of the specific elements that came together to give rise to this particular story.

1. *Seeing pictures.* When Lewis was just a teenager, the picture of a faun carrying an umbrella and packages in the midst of a snowy wood first popped into his mind. Exactly what triggered this image is uncertain, but we do know that it stayed in his imagination well into his adulthood, until he eventually incorporated it into the early scene where Lucy meets Mr. Tumnus in the woods. The "seeing" of imaginary pictures certainly became a familiar literary prompt in Lewis's experience: he later acknowledged that such images were the imaginative spur which encouraged him to write each one of his seven Narnian tales, as well as his three science fiction novels.

2. *Dreams.* Imaginative images not only came to Lewis while he was awake; they also appeared to him when he was sleeping. In particular, in regard to *The Lion, the Witch and the Wardrobe,* while he was in the early stages of writing the story, he had frequent dreams of lions. Then, one day, without any intentionality on his part, Lewis found that Aslan had entered the tale and taken on the role of the story's main protagonist: "At first I had very little idea how the story would go. But then suddenly Aslan came bounding into

it. I think I had been having a good many dreams of lions about that time. Apart from that, I don't know where the Lion came from or why He came. But once He was there He pulled the six other Narnian stories in after Him."

3. *Filling in the gaps in the story.* Having once received these "pictures," Lewis needed to decide what to do with them. Fortunately, he describes this aspect of his creative process in some detail:

> In a certain sense, I have never exactly "made" a story. With me the process is much more like bird-watching than like either talking or building. I see pictures. Some of these pictures have a common flavour, almost a common smell, which groups them together. Keep quiet and watch and they will begin joining themselves up. If you were very lucky (I have never been as lucky as all that) a whole set might join themselves so consistently that there you had a complete story, without doing anything yourself. But more often (in my experience always) there are gaps. Then at last you have to do some deliberate inventing, have to contrive reasons why these characters should be in these various places doing these various things. I have no idea whether this is the usual way of writing stories, still less whether it is the best. It is the only one I know: images always come first.

In the particular instance of *The Lion, the Witch and the Wardrobe,* the filling in of the gaps did not begin to occur until Lewis was in his forties. His biographers Roger Lancelyn Green and Walter Hooper date the very preliminary stages of the Narnian stories to late 1939. There are various reasons they believe this to be true: a few handwritten fragments related to Narnia that survived by happenstance and were intermingled with other of Lewis's manuscript notes dating from this approximate period; the arrival of evacuee children at Lewis's home, The Kilns, in September 1939; and finally and most significantly, Lewis's own statement that he began to write about the image of the faun in a snowy woods when he was "about forty" (his fortieth birthday was November 29, 1938).

EARLY EFFORTS AT CHILDREN'S STORIES

How far these early efforts progressed we do not know. What we do know is that sometime prior to 1947, Lewis completed at least one ill-fated children's story that was not received well by his friends and that he subsequently destroyed. The next hint regarding the literary lineage of the Narnian stories comes from a comment made by Chad Walsh about his visit to Lewis in August 1948. Walsh recalls that Lewis spoke "vaguely of completing a children's book which he has begun 'in the tradition of E. Nesbit.'" We learn elsewhere that this early effort was indeed *The Lion, the Witch and the Wardrobe:* "This [comment by Walsh] referred to the first few chapters of *The Lion, the Witch and the Wardrobe,* a story which had been forming in [Lewis's] mind for some time, but of which only a little had been written down [after being] set aside owing to criticism from one of his older friends."

It is evident that Lewis was finding it somewhat challenging to "fill in the gaps" in the creation of his first children's story. The narrative he began sometime around 1938-1939 was not in fact completed until the spring of 1949—a long gestation process for a writer who typically worked rapidly. Perhaps this creative difficulty was only to be expected, for as much as Lewis loved and read fairy tales, this was nonetheless a new style of writing for him and required a different approach.

THE ASSISTANCE OF ROGER LANCELYN GREEN

In meeting this challenge, it was Lewis's friend Roger Lancelyn Green who proved to be the most helpful in both encouraging and shaping his efforts at crafting a successful children's tale. First of all, Green provided a creative stimulus when he shared with Lewis an unpublished children's story he had written titled "The Wood That Time Forgot." Lewis kept the manuscript of this story for a twelve-month period, from September 1945 to September 1946, when he returned it to Green with his enthusiastic endorsement along with suggestions for revisions.

Those who have read the still unpublished "The Wood That Time Forgot" detect narrative elements that are clearly reminiscent of aspects of Lewis's own later work. For example, it is set in an Oxfordshire wood and includes a temptation sequence where a seemingly kindly old man gives one of the children a sweet-tasting cordial that converts them to the enemy's cause.

LITERARY INFLUENCES

Does this similarity of detail between Lewis's story and Green's unpublished manuscript mean that *The Lion, the Witch and the Wardrobe* was not "original"? Is Lewis, in fact, guilty of something like plagiarism whenever his story echoes (no matter how faintly) some fairy tale that he had read prior to writing his own book? The author of "The Wood That Time Forgot" (from whom Lewis apparently "borrowed") gives a resounding no to this question, declaring that Lewis was not only a myth-maker but also a "myth-user"—a trait of all good authors. In other words, Lewis, who read widely in many different sources, was able to imaginatively combine varied literary influences in a way that ultimately resulted in his own *original* tale.

Literary borrowing is an inevitable part of being a writer; indeed, it is impossible for well-read authors to escape the influence of the books they have already encountered. And, we might well argue, we would not even want to do so, as one of the primary purposes of reading is to be influenced by the text. The question of genuine creativity instead comes down to whether the writer successfully assimilates this source material and truly makes it his or her own rather than just a pale copy. As Green explains in terms of Lewis's children's stories:

> [A rich] background of thought is apparent throughout the Narnia stories, and for this reason it is of little importance to look for "sources" and "originals." Such research might tell us what books Lewis had read, and where some of his ideas came from: but pure invention is almost impossible, and all authors receive their inspiration with the aid of suggestions or trains of thought induced by the odd

word, line, sentence or even idea in another man's book—or in the general background of myth from which as often as not the previous writer himself had drawn. What matters is the use made of these hints, ideas and inspirations—these pieces of coloured glass in the kaleidoscope, which are the old, universal pieces, but now arranged in a new pattern. Lewis's use of myth in making his new mythology covers all such "borrowings" and turns them to glorious account.

THE INFLUENCE OF E. NESBIT'S STORIES

Beyond Green's story, other literary antecedents are readily apparent in *The Lion, the Witch and the Wardrobe* and undoubtedly aided Lewis in his writing process. Classical mythic references (such as the fauns, centaurs and giants), as well as the character of Father Christmas, are indebted to other tales. But most notable among these influences are the writings of E. Nesbit, an author whom Lewis had greatly loved as a child and continued to read as an adult. In comparing the two authors, it becomes apparent that bits and pieces of the Nesbit tales surfaced in Lewis's memory as he was writing and were utilized in his Narnian stories.

In the case of *The Lion, the Witch and the Wardrobe,* the most obvious source of literary influence is Nesbit's "The Aunt and Amabel." In this short story, the young girl Amabel enters another world by the same means as the Pevensie children: through a wardrobe. Even more striking a parallel is the face that Nesbit's wardrobe is an entryway to a magical train station known as "Bigwardrobeinspareroom." Readers of Lewis's *The Lion, the Witch and the Wardrobe* will undoubtedly be reminded of Mr. Tumnus's initial confusion when he understands Lucy to have come from the city of "War Drobe" in the faraway country of "Spare Oom." As obvious as this parallel may be, Lewis himself did not remember having read "The Aunt and Amabel." Thus in this instance the literary influence was subconscious though real. When Green later pointed out the distinct resemblance between this Nesbit story and Lewis's own story, Lewis was quick to grant that he must have read it, though he had long since forgotten the story. Lewis did recognize that his Narnian story overall was influenced by the tales of E. Nesbit and was happy to acknowledge this debt (see comment to Chad Walsh, cited above under "Early Efforts").

THE STORY IS WRITTEN AND OTHERS BEGUN

As significant an impact as these literary influences may have had on Lewis's creative mind, there is no doubt that the original pictures he had "seen"— such as a faun in a snowy wood carrying an umbrella and parcels—and his dreams of lions were the most critical elements sparking his desire to write a children's story. But in spite of this promising beginning, Lewis was uncertain as to how he should proceed. As noted earlier, at this point Green's encouragement proved to be critical. Another close friend, J. R. R. Tolkien, had very much disliked the early chapters of *The Lion, the Witch and the Wardrobe* when Lewis had read them to him. In March 1949, after dining with Roger Green at Magdalen College, Lewis read his guest several chapters of the unfinished tale and then asked him a question: was the story any good? Fortunately for those who have grown to love the Narnian tales, the answer was reassuringly positive, and Lewis continued to write, completing *The Lion, the Witch and the Wardrobe* by the end of that month.

Throughout the composition process, Lewis continued to interact with Green as his most trusted critic. There were points at which they disagreed (this will be touched upon in chapter twenty, "Reception History of *The Lion, the Witch and The Wardrobe*"), but primarily Green provided Lewis with enthusiastic encouragement coupled with minor suggestions "ranging from the deletion of [the word] 'Crikey!' as a common exclamation among the young . . . to the omission of bird's-nesting from among the Pevensie children's occupations, Lewis being unaware of the revolution against 'egg-collectors'" that had by then occurred in British society.

Shortly after his completion of the manuscript of *The Lion, the Witch and the Wardrobe,* Lewis began to write a second children's story, this one about the origins of Narnia. This effort was not successful, however, and was eventually set aside, only to reappear five years later in a much-altered state as *The Magician's Nephew*. In the meantime, Lewis did not give up on the writing of children's stories. He soon found another idea to pursue, and this tale of children pulled unexpectedly into Narnia developed into his second volume, *Prince Caspian*, which was finished by December 1949.

AN ILLUSTRATOR IS CHOSEN

Meanwhile, the publication process was going forward on the first story. Aware of Pauline Baynes's wonderful work for Tolkien's book *Farmer Giles of Ham* (published in 1949), Lewis invited this young artist to illustrate *The Lion, the Witch and the Wardrobe*. She later explained her sense of how the invitation came her way: "C. S. Lewis told me that he had actually gone into a bookshop and asked the assistant there if she could recommend someone who could draw children and animals. I don't know whether he was just being kind to me and making me more important than I was or whether he'd simply heard about me from his friend Tolkien."

Impressed with the excellent work she did for his first story, Lewis eventually asked that she illustrate all seven of his *Narnian Chronicles*. Baynes consulted with Lewis at various points while she was creating the illustrations, and she later described him as

> the most kindly and tolerant of authors—who seemed happy to leave everything in my completely inexperienced hands! Once or twice I queried the sort of character he had in mind—as with Puddleglum—& then he replied, but otherwise he made no remarks or criticisms. . . . I had rather the feeling that, having got the story written down & out of his mind, that the rest was someone else's job, & that he wouldn't interfere.

In the minds of many readers of the Narnian books, the illustrations of Pauline Baynes have become inextricably intertwined with the words of C. S.

Lewis. Her exquisite drawings have undoubtedly contributed to the success of the series by enhancing the wonder of the stories for countless readers.

THE OTHER NARNIAN STORIES ARE WRITTEN

With the illustrator selected and the first two books completed by the end of December 1949, Lewis continued his rather rapid production of additional stories about the land of Narnia. In fact, *The Voyage of the "Dawn Treader"* was finished by the end of February 1950, and "before [that] year was out he had written *The Silver Chair* and *The Horse and His Boy* and made a start on *The Magician's Nephew*. The final installment, *The Last Battle,* was written two years later." *The Magician's Nephew* took much longer to compose than the others and was the last book to be completed, though it was eventually published a year before *The Last Battle*. While Lewis was writing the books he stayed in close touch with Green, meeting with him as regularly as circumstances permitted to read and discuss each story line as it unfolded.

People often wonder whether Lewis intended to write other Narnian tales when he began writing *The Lion, the Witch and the Wardrobe*. In a letter to a reader, Lewis himself answered this decisively: "When I wrote the *Lion* I had no notion of writing the others." Aside from Lewis himself, the one who was closest to the composition process was clearly Green, and he sheds some additional light on this issue. While confirming that Lewis had no intention of writing additional stories when he began, Green does acknowledge that the possibility of a sequel began to surface in a vague way in Lewis's mind as he neared the end of his first Narnian book. Nonetheless, it is clear that Lewis did not begin with a master plan that included a plot outline for additional books. His initial intention was simply to see if he could succeed at producing a good children's story.

Why is it important to answer this question of authorial intent? Because when we look at the subsequent books, it becomes readily apparent that at least one significant contradiction occurs between statements made in *The Lion, the Witch and the Wardrobe* and details given later in *The Magician's Nephew*. In the first book, we are told that the four Pevensie children were the first "Sons of Adam and Daughters of Eve" to have entered Narnia. (See Mr. Beaver's statement "There's never been any of your race here before" [*LWW*, ch. 8, p. 81].) But by the time Lewis wrote *The Magician's Nephew* (the prequel to *The Lion, the Witch and the Wardrobe*) he was backed into a corner by his earlier statements; for not only do Digory and Polly visit Narnia at the time of its creation, but the very first king and queen of this new world also come from London. Hence "Sons of Adam and Daughters of Eve" have visited Narnia from the very first. It is unlikely that this significant contradiction would have occurred if Lewis had anticipated the way his Narnian series would eventually unfold.

Lewis does slip into other inconsistencies from time to time in the books, but they are less important. For example, the invisibility or noninvisibility of objects while in the hands of the Dufflepuds varies in *The Voyage of the "Dawn Treader"*: contrast the invisibility of the spear with the visibility of the dishes of food, even though Lewis states plainly that objects become visible only when they leave the hands of the Dufflepuds.

SUMMARY OF PUBLICATION HISTORY

By the end of March 1950, illustrations for *The Lion, the Witch and the Wardrobe* were being produced, while staff of the publisher, Geoffrey Bles, were busy creating the dust jacket. By June 22, final proofs were being read. The book was issued in hardback by the British publisher on October 16, 1950, with the first American edition published on November 7 by Macmillan in New York.

This book and the other six Narnian volumes have been continuously in print ever since they were first published. This fact alone is a remarkable publishing feat. Given the great number of volumes published since the series inception (sales for all seven books combined currently surpass 3.5 million annually, with a total estimated sales of 85 million since the first volume was published in 1950) and the thirty-three languages into which the books have been translated, it is clear that the seven Chronicles of Narnia are not only enduring classics in the field of children's literature but a publishing phenomenon as well.

Publication Timeline

Creation of *The Lion, the Witch and the Wardrobe* and Publication of the Other Narnian Tales

1939	Lewis makes his first tentative attempts to write a children's story
August 1948	Chad Walsh learns that Lewis is writing a story in the "tradition of E. Nesbit"
March 10, 1949	Roger Lancelyn Green encourages Lewis to continue writing the story
end of March 1949	*The Lion, the Witch and the Wardrobe* is finished
December 1949	Lewis meets his chosen illustrator, Pauline Baynes
June 22, 1950	Proofs of the story are being read
October 16, 1950	*The Lion, the Witch and the Wardrobe* is published in hardback by Geoffrey Bles (London)
November 7, 1950	*The Lion, the Witch and the Wardrobe* is published in hardback by Macmillan (New York)
October 1951	*Prince Caspian* is published in hardback in London by Geoffrey Bles and in New York by Macmillan
September 1952	*The Voyage of the "Dawn Treader"* is published in hardback in London by Geoffrey Bles and in New York by Macmillan
September 1953	*The Silver Chair* is published in hardback in London by Geoffrey Bles
October 1953	*The Silver Chair* is published in New York by Macmillan
September 1954	*The Horse and His Boy* is published in hardback in London by Geoffrey Bles
October 1954	*The Horse and His Boy* is published in New York by Macmillan
May 1955	*The Magician's Nephew* is published in hardback in London by the Bodley Head
October 1955	*The Magician's Nephew* is published in New York by Macmillan
March 1956	*The Last Battle* is published in hardback in London by the Bodley Head
September 1956	*The Last Battle* is published by Macmillan in New York

20

Reception History of
The Lion, the Witch and the Wardrobe

In the decades since *The Lion, the Witch and the Wardrobe* was first published, critical response to C. S. Lewis's seven children's stories has been both vigorous and diverse. In particular, adult readers of the Chronicles of Narnia have tended to respond to these works with either passionate appreciation or extreme hostility. By and large, there appears to be very little middle ground. Why is this so? What does this intensity of varied response tell us about the story? What does it say about what Lewis was attempting to accomplish? Even more, what does it tell us about whether he succeeded in his goals as an author?

CRITICS: PRO AND CON

Before we can begin to answer these questions, we need to acquaint ourselves with a brief overview of the critical commentary. We will begin with those who view the Chronicles of Narnia with high approval, making favorable statements such as the following:

> [The Narnian books] are the best-known and most influential works
> of a well-known and very influential writer. . . . Regarded as classics
> by many authorities on children's literature, they are read and loved
> also by college students and older adults. (Peter J. Schakel)

> In spite of anything that can be said against them, and considering *The
> Chronicles of Narnia* as dispassionately as possible, it seems safe to say
> that C. S. Lewis has earned by them a place among the greatest writers

of children's books and—surprising as it would have seemed to him—he will probably be remembered for them more than for anything else he wrote. (Roger Lancelyn Green and Walter Hooper)

It is an irony of literary history. This man, who wrote the most glittering religious apologetics of his time, and who was a major literary historian, may well have created his most lasting work in seven fairy tales nominally for children. (Chad Walsh)

In contrast to those who speak appreciatively of the books, there are those who harshly condemn them. Not only do these negative critics see little merit in the Narnian tales, but they often react violently against them:

However innocent its beginnings, the story of Narnia was animated by one compelling need. . . . It was not a need to reveal Christ to children but to have a place where Lewis could pass judgement on people with impunity. *The Chronicles*, after all, are exactly that, the story of a world created and a world destroyed, with some saved and many damned. It was a poor enough choice of subject for a children's parable. . . . Any scribe foolhardy enough to attempt it must at least take care to recognize in himself and edit out any baser instincts that might compromise the work. The humility to do this is what is so lacking in the Apocalypse According to Saint Jack. Lewis was as empty of true sympathies as he was full of shabby opinions. (John Goldthwaite)

In order to understand the meaning of such fantasies as the "Narnia" books . . . I believe we have to go back to the very early days in the author's life . . . [and] we have to attend to meanings to be found in the work itself, especially in its symbolism. When we do this, we find themes in the "Narnia" books that would seem to belong to a profound state of insecurity and dread. As I have said, the world of Lewis's fantasies and his view of the "real" world are paranoid-schizoid. (David Holbrook)

> There is no doubt in the public mind that what matters [in terms of
> Lewis's works] is the Narnia cycle, and that is where the puzzle comes,
> because there is no doubt in my mind that it is one of the most ugly
> and poisonous things I've ever read. (Philip Pullman)

No middle ground indeed! There are exceptions to these general categories, of course, but we will begin our review of the critical commentary by
focusing on the latter of these two extremes: negative critics who find little
of worth in the Narnian books and often regard them as potentially destruc-
tive. Not all of the issues they raise are necessarily present in *The Lion, the
Witch and the Wardrobe,* but they are all criticisms that have been leveled at
the series as a whole.

THE HOSTILE VOICES

The best known of Lewis's Narnian critics is himself an accomplished, best-
selling children's author, Englishman Philip Pullman. Ironically, there are
certain similarities between the imaginary worlds these writers have created,
but there are also crucial differences. A website encyclopedia summaries
their likenesses as follows: "The two series resemble each other in many
ways. Both feature pre-adolescent children facing adult moral choices, talking animals, religious allegories, parallel worlds, and the fate of the worlds
hanging in the balance. The first published *Narnia* book . . . starts with a
young girl hiding in a wardrobe, as does [Pullman's] first *Dark Materials*
book, *Northern Lights.*" Gregg Easterbrook, writing in the *Atlantic Monthly,*
offers this view of the comparisons and contrasts: "Both Lewis's and Pullman's series take place on earth and in a parallel world; both have as protag-
onists astonishingly capable children; and the subtext of both is the search
for the divine. But in Lewis's books children seek the divine in order to experience happiness and perfect love, whereas in Pullman's trilogy they seek
it in order to destroy it." Finally, Peter Hitchens, a conservative columnist
who writes for the *Spectator* (and is a critic of Pullman's attacks on Lewis),

adds his understanding of several of the contrasts between these two worlds:

> Pullman's stories are crammed with the supernatural and the mystical, and take place mainly in alternative worlds, most captivatingly of all in Oxford recognisably the same place while utterly different. But while Narnia is under the care of a benevolent, kindly creator, Pullman's chaotic universe has no ultimate good authority, controlling and redeeming all. God, or someone claiming to be God, dies meaninglessly in the third volume of this trilogy.

Thus in spite of some surface similarities, it is apparent that there are great differences between Pullman's stories and Lewis's—differences that Pullman himself would underscore and applaud.

In their understanding of the creative process, however, there are a few points of contact between these two talented authors. For example, in a biographical piece that Pullman wrote for his young readers, he explains: "I was sure that I was going to write stories myself when I grew up. It's important to put it like that—not 'I'm a writer,' but rather 'I write stories.' If you put the emphasis on yourself rather than your work, you're in danger of thinking that you're the most important thing. But you're not. The story is what matters, and you're only the servant, and your job is to get it out on time and in good order." The vocabulary differs, but Lewis would have agreed that the focus properly remains on the writing of a good story rather than on the person of the author.

Pullman acknowledges such literary commonalities, in spite of his disdain for the Narnian stories: "To be sure, there is something to be said for [Lewis]. The literary criticism is, at the very least, effortlessly readable . . . [and] he says some things about myth and fairy tale and writing for children which are both true and interesting." But once we get beyond this point and begin to delve into the underlying philosophical and religious beliefs of these popular children's authors, we are once again made aware of the massive and irreconcilable divide between the two.

Unfortunately, in a brief guide of this sort, we do not have the space to fully address the criticisms that Pullman and others raise. Certainly their critiques deserve a more developed response than we are able to provide, and we look forward to the work of others who will be able to engage more completely with the arguments of these critics. Here we will simply raise their basic criticisms and attempt to help you, the reader, see how these charges might be answered.

The charge of racism. Some of those who dislike the Chronicles of Narnia do so because they perceive intolerant attitudes, including racism, within the stories. Is this accurate? Was Lewis guilty of racism in his writing? Some say yes, noting that in the Narnian tales many of Lewis's villains are dark-skinned Calormenes.

Others respond that this charge is baseless: they point to the evil character of the White Witch (certainly she does not have a dark complexion) and to the worthy Calormene Emeth in *The Last Battle*. Neither of these key examples fits the pattern of an overt racial prejudice. Peter Schakel underscores this point by reminding readers that Lewis was writing within a traditional literary convention, the romance story (see chapter twelve for more on this literary genre). Schakel concludes:

> One may well regret the emphasis on the dark skins and garlicy breath of the Calormenes and the dwarfs' references to the Calormenes as "Darkies." But the Calormenes are not simply "dark persons"—they are Moors: they are identified by their dress, weapons, and manners as the traditional enemy in medieval romances. More important, however, than Lewis's use of this convention are his frequent departures from and adaptations of it.

Other authors share Schakel's discomfort over certain word choices, but they do not believe these choices indicate unabashed racism. As Gregg Easterbrook explains:

> I have three children, aged six to twelve, and a few months ago I fin-

ished reading the *Chronicles* to them. Even as a fan I must admit that certain passages made me wince. For example, the wicked dwarfs ridicule the Calormenes as "darkies"; I skirted the word, because I don't want it in my kids' heads. But does having characters say "darkies" make Lewis racist? He was, after all, employing language then in common parlance—and placing it in the mouths of the wicked. "Many older books contain race or gender differences discordant to modern ears," John G. West Jr., a co-editor of *The C. S. Lewis Encyclopedia*, told me recently. "We don't stop reading Twain or Darwin because they used racial terms no author uses today."

The charge of misogyny. Questions about Lewis's attitudes toward women have also been raised by some readers of the Narnian books and other of his fictional works as well. What of this charge? Is it fair to say that Lewis disliked or even hated women generally?

Many examples from his personal life strongly contradict this accusation. A lifelong bachelor until he married Joy Davidman when he was in his late fifties, Lewis didn't always feel completely comfortable around women. His closest friends were male, yet he did have close friendships with several intelligent, accomplished women, among them the poet Ruth Pitter and the Anglican nun Sister Penelope. In addition, there are numerous documented examples of the courtesy, kindness and respect he demonstrated to his female pupils. Lewis's acknowledged preference for male company did frequently result in the exclusion of females (such as Tolkien's wife) from social settings, and certain recorded comments (both written and spoken) suggest a strong male bias. But none of this amounts to a hatred of women: chauvinism perhaps, gender bias at times, sexism maybe, but not misogyny.

In the Narnian stories, the charges of misogyny primarily result from Lewis's portrayal of Susan, who is reported in the final book, *The Last Battle,* as being "no longer a friend of Narnia . . . she's interested in nothing nowadays except nylons and lipstick and invitations. She was always a jolly sight too keen on being grown-up" (chap. 12). As Pullman rather sweepingly con-cludes: "Susan like Cinderella, is undergoing a transition from one phase of her life to another. Lewis didn't approve of that. He didn't like women in general, or sexuality at all, at least at the stage when he wrote the Narnia books. He was appalled and frightened at the notion of wanting to grow up."

Still other critics point to the traditional roles assigned to Lewis's charac-ters—the female children are the ones who nurture and care for others, while the male characters mainly (though not exclusively) assume the task of protection and fighting in physical battles—as evidence of his chauvinis-tic sexism.

The author of a website devoted to discussing Pullman's anti-Lewis rhet-oric advises that we need to remember that Lewis was writing in a different day from ours and also employing the chivalric standard of the medieval pe-riod in his fiction:

> Lewis certainly had a different view of women from what is commonly accepted today, but that is not the same as being "disparaging of girls and women." How could his view not be different? He was writing fifty years ago. Not only that, but he was a professor of Mediaeval lit-erature, saturated in the knightly ideals of honor and valor. Of course his view of women was different than ours. Lewis was a child of his time; just as Pullman is a child of his. In fifty years, what will people criticize Philip Pullman for?

Other authors counter the negative portrayal of Susan by pointing out that her sister Lucy is the one who most often sees Aslan and is clearly re-garded with approval and fondness by Lewis the author.

Given this brief survey, it would appear that labeling Lewis an outright mi-sogynist on the basis of his children's stories is an unfair and exaggerated re-sponse. Nonetheless, some who genuinely enjoy and value the writings of Lewis (including the Narnian stories) still question certain of his gender atti-tudes. Those who wish to explore this topic further will find a helpful overview in *Women Among the Inklings* by Candice Fredrick and Sam McBride. The authors identify themselves as being both Christians and feminists (designations that they acknowledge to be most often viewed as contradictory, not complementary). Undoubtedly, many readers of Lewis will not agree with all conclusions of these authors, but even those who disagree completely with their analysis will still benefit from a more thoughtful engagement with this issue. It should also be noted that even though they strongly differ with Lewis on gender issues, Fredrick and McBride balance this disagreement with an affirmation that the flaws they perceive in Lewis do "not in any way negate his literary accomplishments and work as a Christian apologist."

The charge of excessive violence and hatred. Other critics struggle with the fact that there are violent battles in the Narnian stories. They object to the fact that children are involved in the fighting and that at times Aslan himself leads the struggle. One critic is particularly scathing in his rejection of the final scene in *The Silver Chair,* when Aslan sends Jill and Eustace (along with the Narnian King Caspian) back to the horrid school in their own world to teach the bullies there a lesson by giving them a taste of their own medicine. As John Goldthwaite angrily expounds:

> Lewis titled this satisfying little episode "The Healing of Harms." But what Christ is it that heals with the sword? It can hardly obtain that the recipients of this schoolyard justice are themselves bullies or that no one actually gets gut-stuck in the melee. The matter here is that Christian teaching has reverted to the Dirty Harry theology of the *lex talionis,* an eye for an eye and a tooth for a tooth. Lewis has contrived a Christ willing to turn his back while his chosen children, in the name of vengeance, beat up another group of children. . . . Whatever a Christian's personal lapses, pacifism is an ideal that he is bound by faith to honor whether it suits him or not. To scorn it before children is corrupt. . . . What Lewis here wants his prerogative audience to sanction is the notion that violence, being intrinsic to man's nature, is

permissible if conducted properly—under civilized rules, against mutually agreed upon enemies, preferably by knights—rather than being the sorriest of all specimens of original sin. What we see him doing at the end of *The Silver Chair* is really quite stunning. I cannot imagine a betrayal of one's faith more complete than this last picture of Christ at the playground, putting weapons into the hands of children.

More moderate critics address this question of violence by examining it within the literary genre of the Narnian tales. Here is Schakel's take:

There is violence in the *Chronicles:* it is part of the romance tradition Lewis was using. But there is less violence than one would expect if Lewis were closely following the romance convention, with its tendency toward sudden, barely motivated violence: three books . . . contain very little violence at all. When violence does appear in the other books, it is used as a metaphor, as battles against evil, which is strong and aggressive and must be resisted actively. . . . But it is most significant that the *Chronicles* do not follow the typical romance in presenting strength as the way to solve problems. The good side in Narnia is always the weaker side. . . . Victory for the Narnians comes only through Aslan.

Critics such as Schakel do not believe the Narnian stories glorify violence, nor that Lewis intended them to do so. Instead, the warfare in the Narnian books is clearly the result of evil, and utilized only as a last resort to protect the weak and to restore the good.

The charge of occult influence. While the prior three concerns (sexism, racism and excessive violence) are voiced by both secular and Christian critics, this fourth charge is primarily issued by conservative Christians who are concerned over what they perceive as a promotion of occult practices within the Narnian stories. In her website article "C. S. Lewis: The Devil's Wisest Fool," Mary Van Nattan is blunt in her indictment of Narnia as dangerous and even anti-Christian:

The Chronicles of Narnia are one of the most powerful tools of Satan
that Lewis ever produced. Worst of all, these books are geared toward
children. . . . As we study the *Chronicles of Narnia,* the dark and ugly
truth will come to light. We will find that the symbolism that he used
and things he included in the stories are extremely blasphemous. In
the end he is casting the truth of God as the same as and the fulfillment
of paganism and witchcraft.

Given the large number of Christian readers who find great truth and
value in these stories, most readers do not share Van Nattan's view of the occult orientation of the Narnian tales. Once again, Schakel offers helpful
words to shed light on this issue:

Lewis did not share a concern some parents and religious leaders
have about what they regard as a dangerous misuse of imagination—
that is the use of witches and magic in his *Chronicles of Narnia.* . . .
[He used them] in the *Chronicles* because they are an integral characteristic of the genre in which he was writing, the fairy tale. This in itself is not an adequate defense, of course, to those who would object
to reading all fairy tales on the same grounds, as unedifying and non-
Christian. Within the tradition Lewis was drawing on, however,
witches are the evil characters in stories depicting good and evil in
black and white terms.

For a further discussion of magic and *The Lion, the Witch and the Wardrobe,*
see our section on Harry Potter and the Narnian tales in chapter thirteen.

Criticisms of the literary quality of the Narnian tales. Some critiques of the
Narnian books are not philosophical in nature but rather evaluate Lewis's
success as an author in creating a good story. Sadly, one of Lewis's closest
friends, fellow fantasy writer J. R. R. Tolkien, very much disliked the Narnian stories, finding them inconsistent in their mythology and plot. After
hearing *The Lion, the Witch and the Wardrobe* read while it was still in manuscript form, Tolkien commented to a mutual friend, Roger L. Green: "I hear

you've been reading Jack's children's story. It really won't do, you know! I mean to say: *'Nymphs and their Ways, The Love-Life of a Faun.'* Doesn't he know what he is talking about?" Tolkien's criticisms of the story were quite devastating and hurt Lewis a great deal.

Fortunately, there were other friends who valued the first Narnian story and encouraged Lewis's efforts (see chapter eighteen). An appreciative critic of the Narnian tales overall, Roger Green still saw minor flaws in the book. For example, he originally agreed with Tolkien that the arrival of Father Christmas struck a jarring note in the first story (Green later moderated his view on this point). Another friend, poet Ruth Pitter, recalled with pleasure her good-natured "win" over Lewis, when she caught him in a textual error in *The Lion, the Witch and the Wardrobe:* where did the Beavers obtain certain foodstuffs (e.g., potatoes, flour, sugar, oranges, milk) for the dinner they provided for the Pevensie children, given that it was winter and (by Lewis's own setup of the story) no foreign trade was allowed? According to Pitter's memory of the conversation, Lewis had no answer and was "stumped."

REVIEWS OF THE NARNIAN BOOKS

In terms of early published reviews, Lewis's biographers, Green and Hooper, state that "the critical reception of the seven books was varied and usually guarded. But the reader's reception both in Great Britain and the United States, if slow at first, was enthusiastic." A sampling of comments from these reviews follows:

> The *Chronicles of Narnia* are fine heroic tales. In children's books, one may be tempted to think, the almost lost art of narrative is kept alive; certainly Professor Lewis tells a story as few adult romancers can. . . . What makes the "Narnia" stories stand out from the dreary grey mass of much contemporary writing for children is not good style or vivid characterization or even superb story-telling, but the fact that the author has something to say. (Marcus S. Crouch, *Junior Bookshelf,* 1956)

[The Lion, the Witch and the Wardrobe] is, in turn, beautiful, frightening, wise, and nonsensical, and should captivate, with or without its parable, the right child of between eight and eleven years old. (New Yorker, 1950)

[The Lion, the Witch and the Wardrobe] is all a beautifully written, modern parable, perhaps doing for our times what George MacDonald tried to do for his. (Louise S. Bechtel, New York Herald Tribune Book Review, 1950)

[The Lion, the Witch and the Wardrobe] tells of the struggle between good and evil in terms that make it a dramatic story. . . . It is an exceptionally good new "fairy tale." (Mary Gould Davis, Saturday Review, 1950)

[In The Lion, the Witch and the Wardrobe] Lewis transmutes romantic longing into an imaginative fulfillment which "is in itself the very reverse of wishful thinking; it is more like thoughtful wishing." He extrapolates Christian tradition into another dimension, one just around the corner from us in time and space. (Charles A. Brady, Buffalo Evening News, 1950)

The whole air of [The Lion, the Witch and the Wardrobe] is rich and strange and coherent; there is something of Hans Andersen's power to move and George MacDonald's power to create strange worlds, and it is, naturally, beautifully written. (Guardian, 1951)

For children, the inner meaning of [the Chronicles of Narnia] may be only dimly understood, or understood imaginatively rather than intellectually; but few children can remain unmoved by the magnificent scenes of action, or the lively and odd characters, or the wonderful timing of suspense and climax, or the colourful and romantic settings. At a time when narrative is in general the weakest feature of contemporary fiction, Dr. Lewis shows in the Narnia stories that he is a storyteller in the authentic tradition. (Chosen for Children, 1967)

CHILDREN'S RESPONSES TO THE NARNIAN BOOKS

In this chapter thus far, we have been dealing with adult critical response, but what of Lewis's child readers? Until recent years, with the arrival of the Internet and its numerous book review sites (see, for example, www.spaghettibookclub.org for a sampling of children's reviews), children rarely had opportunities to publicly evaluate books they had read. Further, more often than issuing a negative review, a child's typical reaction to a story he or she does not like is simply to stop reading. Obviously, this type of negative response is difficult to quantify, but gauging the reverse is somewhat easier. The fact that the Narnian books have remained continuously in print since they were first published, decades ago, speaks loudly to their favorable reception—as does the impressive number of copies sold worldwide (estimated eighty five million total sales for the seven volumes). Clearly, if children were not enjoying the books, sales of this magnitude would not have endured.

Francis Spufford, an English journalist and critic, first read the Narnian stories as a young boy growing up in Keele, England. Not without his criticisms of these stories, he nonetheless retains a sense of what so captivated him as a child reading the Chronicles of Narnia. Reflecting back on this childhood experience, Spufford affectionately recalls:

> The books I loved best of all took me away through a wardrobe, and a shallow pool in the grass of a sleepy orchard, and a picture in a frame, and a door in a garden wall on a rainy day at boarding school, and always to Narnia. Other imaginary countries interested me, beguiled me, made rich suggestions to me. Narnia made me feel like I'd taken hold of a live wire. The book in my hand sent jolts and shimmers through my nerves. It affected me bodily. In Narnia, C. S. Lewis invented objects for my longing, gave forms to my longing, that I would never have thought of, and yet they seemed exactly right: he had anticipated what would delight me with an almost unearthly intimacy. Immediately I discovered them, they became the inevitable ex-

pressions of my longing. So from the moment I first encountered *The Lion, the Witch and the Wardrobe* to when I was eleven or twelve, the seven *Chronicles of Narnia* represented essence-of-book to me. . . . For four or five years, I essentially read other books because I could not always be rereading the Narnia books. . . . But in other books, I was always seeking for partial or diluted reminders of Narnia, always hoping for a gleam of the sensation of Narnia. Once felt, never forgotten.

The Christian Vision of
The Lion, the Witch and the Wardrobe

The Lion, the Witch and the Wardrobe is a Christian classic. This concluding chapter is designed to identify the specific things that make the book Christian, and in particular the Christian ideas and ideals embodied in the characters and action. Several preliminaries are important.

First, a Christian work of literature must be a work of literature before it can be a Christian literary work. It must meet the ordinary criteria of literature in order to rank as a piece of literature at all. These literary qualities are the enabling context for the Christian dimension of a work, and Christian readers should feel no hesitation in relishing them for their own sake. For this reason, we will say something in this chapter about the things that make *The Lion, the Witch and the Wardrobe* a refreshing narrative experience for all readers, Christian and non-Christian alike.

Second, ideas and moral ideals can be Christian without being exclusively Christian. Many of the ideas within the Christian faith are ones that Christians share with other religious and ethical viewpoints. Picture two overlapping circles, one representing Christian ideas and the other representing religious and ethical systems. There is a big overlapping area of shared material. We can call the Christian ideas that fall within the overlapping area *inclusively Christian* viewpoints, meaning that they include Christianity and other religious and moral systems. These ideas are no less Christian for not being *exclusively Christian* in their content.

Third, scholars and literary critics have evolved a system of words and categories by which to analyze the intellectual and moral content of a work of literature (as well as other types of writing). All of these are useful. Here is a brief list:

- *Ethos:* a catchall term that encompasses the distinguishing attitudes, habits and ideas of a culture or group, as in Lewis's statement that "to judge between one *ethos* and another, it is necessary to have got inside both, and if literary history does not help us to do so it is a great waste of labour."

- *Worldview or world picture:* a coherent system of beliefs and values, on the basis of which people assimilate their experiences and base their beliefs and actions. Lewis's formula "the habitual furniture of our minds" is one way of picturing a worldview. The furniture of our minds is the system of assumptions about life that is part of our intellectual makeup. We respond to events in life and ideas that we encounter in terms of this collection of beliefs and attitudes.

- *Story material,* or what in the Middle Ages and Renaissance was called the *matter* of a literary work: the literal, surface content we encounter as we read a story, along the lines of Lewis's statement about "the matter of our story," defined as "everything in the story." When Lewis uses the old term *matter* here, he means the plot line, characters and settings out of which a storyteller constructs a story.

- *Morality or moral vision:* the standards that govern how people relate to their fellow humans, or what Lewis in *Mere Christianity* repeatedly calls "the Law of Right and Wrong" (meaning right and wrong behavior).

- *Theme,* sometimes called *the moral* of a story (not to be confused with the moral vision of a story): the ideas about life that are espoused in a work of literature, along the lines of Lewis's advice to storytellers, "Let the pictures tell you their own moral," or his formulation about "the comments on life" that readers deduce from literature. Lewis here refers to the ideas that can be extracted from a story—the beliefs that the storyteller wants the reader to carry away from it.

Although we have not divided the discussion that follows strictly in reference to these categories, they are useful concepts to keep in mind. They are the "terms of engagement" as we explore the Christian vision of *The Lion, the Witch and the Wardrobe*.

THE *LION*, THE *WITCH* AND THE *WARDROBE* AS WHOLESOME ENTERTAINMENT

We can profitably begin at the broadest possible level with the narrative aspects of the story that interest Christian readers, even though they do not directly impinge on Christian doctrine and morality. One of these is the refreshment value of the story. Basing his remark on 1 Corinthians 10:31, with its command "whether you eat or drink, or whatever you do, do all to the glory of God," Lewis claimed that "the Christian . . . has no objection to comedies that merely amuse and tales that merely refresh. . . . We can play, as we can eat, to the glory of God."

Applied to *The Lion, the Witch and the Wardrobe,* this is primarily a comment about how Christian readers might assimilate and experience the work. The important principle is that Christian readers are free to revel in the story qualities of the book, including its fantasy. Francis Schaeffer wrote famously that "Christian artists do not need to be threatened by fantasy and imagination. . . . The Christian is the really free person—he is free to have imagination. . . . The Christian is the one whose imagination should fly beyond the stars."

If we apply the announced topic of this chapter with flexibility, then, part of the Christian vision of *The Lion, the Witch and the Wardrobe* is the opportunity it affords Christian readers to delight in the pleasures of the story. Lewis himself endorsed the hedonistic defense of literature (though that was not the whole of his defense). In a number of different places, Lewis took his stand against a purely didactic (teaching) or utilitarian defense of literature. In one of these places he wrote that "a great deal (not all) of our literature was made to be read lightly, for entertainment. If we do not read it, in a sense, 'for fun' . . . we are not using it as it was meant to be used."

Christian readers have intuitions about the difference between wholesome and unwholesome recreations. Another fruitful line of inquiry, therefore, is what things make *The Lion, the Witch and the Wardrobe* the wholesome entertainment that Christian readers especially have found it to be. For starters: here is a story that does not contain a compulsory sex scene or scene of gratuitous violence, that does not sentimentalize life by ignoring its negative aspects, that makes the good attractive and the evil unattractive, and that obeys time-honored rules of good storytelling and stylistic excellence.

Finally, we can gain a clearer view of the refreshment value of *The Lion, the Witch and the Wardrobe* if we pause to list the kinds or levels of pleasure at which it can be enjoyed. The categories include these:

- the intellectual pleasure of its ideas
- the aesthetic pleasure of its artistic properties
- the emotional refreshment of responding affectively to characters and events
- the pleasures of the imagination (including the fictional imagination and the fantastic imagination)
- the pleasures of words skillfully employed
- spiritual refreshment

Ꮼ *For Reflection or Discussion*

A good way to cast a retrospective look over your reading of the book is to note the ways you found it refreshing and recreative.

- For you personally, what are the notable pleasures of this book?
- What things make the reading of *The Lion, the Witch and the Wardrobe* wholesome recreation? What makes it fun for the whole family?
- While there is no requirement that the pleasures you find in this book be distinctively Christian, you may nonetheless want to reflect on ways you think your enjoyment of the book is distinctively Christian, and as part of that, why the book has appealed more strongly to the Christian public than to a broad cross section of the population.

HUMAN EXPERIENCE IN *THE LION, THE WITCH AND THE WARDROBE*

The issue of wholesome recreation carries over into our consideration of the narrative elements of the story. We need to say at once that the subject matter of literature is not by itself ideationally laden, so that this is not where the Christian dimension of the book is primarily to be located. Still, the very events and images that stories put before us can be either positive or negative in themselves, and part of the wholesomeness of *The Lion, the Witch and the Wardrobe* stems from the groundwork that Lewis assembled as the enabling foundation for what he wanted to say morally and religiously.

Furthermore, the knowledge that literature imparts is in part a knowledge that can be labeled "right seeing." The subject of literature is human experience, and as we assimilate a work of literature, we look closely at the human experiences that the writer has assembled. The wisdom we derive from reading literature is thus partly an understanding of the human condition— an understanding that should be welcomed by Christians even if it is something that they share with non-Christians.

For our purposes, the subject matter of Lewis's story falls into two categories. There are first of all the pleasures of the content that makes up *The Lion, the Witch and the Wardrobe*. We can begin with the genres that converge in the book. For example, *The Lion, the Witch and the Wardrobe* is an adventure story. Entering into the spirit of the adventures of the Pevensie children contributes a sense of what G. K. Chesterton called "the romance of life."

Another genre that accounts for much of the story material we encounter in the book is fantasy. Fantasy, in turn, assumes a level of reality beyond the tangible world around us. We might say that it initiates us every time we read it into an orientation that is quite at odds with the prevailing cultural assumptions around us. Fantasy opens up alternate worlds and makes us distrust the premise that what we see and touch is the only reality. So Christian readers can profitably think about how the basic premises of fantasy literature strengthen their own worldview.

The broader genre of fictional narrative can itself be scrutinized in these terms. Stories whisk us away from our time and place to another time and place. In *The Lion, the Witch and the Wardrobe,* the world that we enter is first of all a quaintly British world. Then when we walk through the wardrobe into Narnia, we enter another world, with *its* unique properties. The result is a tremendous sense of self-transcendence, coupled with the possibility of experiencing the quality that Lewis highly valued in the reading of literature—enlargement of being, as we "see with other eyes, . . . imagine with other imaginations, . . . feel with other hearts, as well as with our own." It can be fruitful to ask, how does the particular kind of self-transcendence we find in reading *The Lion, the Witch and the Wardrobe* contribute to our lives as Christians?

In addition to these matters dealing with the literary forms of Lewis's book, the "matter" of the story consists of the human experiences that make up the story's content. The writer's goal (as Joseph Conrad famously said) is to make us *see.* "Right seeing" is a form of knowledge. When we contemplate something with care, we come to understand it better. We might think of the subject matter of literature in terms of its *putting us in touch with* various aspects of life.

Any anatomy of the experiences we encounter when reading *The Lion, the Witch and the Wardrobe* runs the risk of seeming arbitrary in its selectiveness, so the following should be regarded as a preliminary list. Some of the categories of experience are specifically moral and spiritual, dimensions of the story that we will take up later in this chapter.

One of the most obvious ingredients of the story is family dynamics—specifically, sibling relations. "Once there were four children," we read at the very outset of the story. Thereafter we are scarcely ever *not* aware that these four children are members of the same biological family. As we pursue the relations of the four siblings to each other, we get the good, the bad and the ugly, leading us to be aware that the "right seeing" literature gives us concerns the negative sides of life as well as the positive.

We would not say that *The Lion, the Witch and the Wardrobe* is *about* the natural world, and yet we are rather continuously aware of nature as a prime setting for virtually all the events in the story. We experience the faces of nature in many different forms. Depending on how much attention we wish to give to this aspect of the story, our encounter with nature in the story can heighten our awareness of certain features of our own experience in the world. The story can provide windows into nature, and we can analyze exactly what view of nature we get as we look through those windows. It was in fairy tales, J. R. R. Tolkien said, that he first experienced the power of such things as "stone, and wood, . . . tree and grass."

The Lion, the Witch and the Wardrobe is a book about intergenerational relations between young people and adults. We go through the action from the point of view of the young, but at any point we may experience an event from the perspective of the Professor or Mr. and Mrs. Beaver or Mr. Tumnus. How the young and old relate to each other and the question of what each adds to life are things that the story gets us to ponder and contemplate.

The story is also about power structures, good and bad, and how the lives of all of us are deeply influenced by the powers to whom we are answerable. At some moments in the story power resides in the hands of good characters, and other times in the hands of evil forces. In both instances, the importance of power structures in human experience is highlighted by the story.

Another area of human experience depicted in depth and range in *The Lion, the Witch and the Wardrobe* is childhood. This stems largely from the fact that the lead human characters are four prepubescent children. As we accompany the Pevensies on their adventures, we traverse the heights and depths, the longings and fears, that characterize the experience of children everywhere.

Ꮔ *For Reflection or Discussion*

These categories are only examples; we have put them on the table as prompts to elicit your own examples and understanding. Here are questions that can aid that process.

- How do the genres that converge in *The Lion, the Witch and the Wardrobe*—such as adventure, fantasy and fictional narrative—intersect with the interests and experiences a Christian reader might bring to the experience of reading the book?

- If we adopt the premise that all truth, wisdom and insight are of value to a Christian, what knowledge in the form of "right seeing" most strongly imprints itself in your awareness as you take stock of the human experiences that make up the content of Lewis's story?

- The nineteenth-century French writer Charles Baudelaire bequeathed a great formula when he spoke of stories "in which the deep significance of life reveals itself." What things make up this "deep significance" in *The Lion, the Witch and the Wardrobe?*

- We can also apply a formula of Lewis, who, after cataloging recognizable human experiences in *The Wind in the Willows,* speaks of how an excursion into those imagined experiences "strengthens our relish for real life" and "sends us back with renewed pleasure to the actual." In what ways does *The Lion, the Witch and the Wardrobe* send you back to real life with increased understanding and relish?

THE MORAL VISION OF *THE LION, THE WITCH AND THE WARDROBE*

Morality has to do with human behavior, especially as seen in people's relationships and interaction with other people. Narrative, of course, is inherently and inevitably moral because it portrays people interacting with other people. In addition to *portraying* moral situations, stories also embody moral *viewpoints* and eventually a moral vision. In the formula of novelist Joyce

Cary, stories give us a picture not only of the world but also of what is right and wrong in that world.

Three things determine the moral vision in a work of literature. The least determinative is the subject matter. This component is generally overrated by Christian readers, especially when the subject matter is vulgar or offensive. This is not to say that there is *no* moral dimension to the subject matter of a story, but only that it is not as large a factor as some moralists make it. But that is really irrelevant to *The Lion, the Witch and the Wardrobe.* The subject matter of the story is not immoral, and its potential to elicit moral reflection is high.

The second thing that determines the moral vision of a story is the viewpoint embodied within the story. This leads to an analysis of how a storyteller gets us to approve or disapprove of characters, settings and events. Here we look for devices of disclosure—things that a storyteller puts into a story to guide a reader's response or interpretation. For example, the prolonged scene (chapter 5) in which the professor decisively silences Susan's and Peter's skepticism about whether other worlds exist is a device of disclosure by which Lewis signals his belief in the supernatural. We need to note, though, that storytellers whose viewpoint is moral rather than immoral often pay their readers the compliment of assuming that *their* moral sense, too, is healthy and capable of sensing what characters and events are worthy of approval and disapproval.

The largest determinant of whether a given reader's experience of a story is moral is the response of the reader herself or himself. What matters most is what happens within the individual reader during and after the reading experience. Even works that espouse an immoral viewpoint can be assimilated in a moral way by readers who exert their own moral viewpoint in the face of the contrary data and viewpoint endorsed by the story. Thus the moral sense that a reader carries *to* the reading experience is crucial. The ultimate test of the morality of a story is what a reader does with the story.

We have discussed how we can tell whether a story is moral or immoral. But what things actually make up the moral vision of a story? How can we determine what the morality of a story is?

Morality is a matter of behavior, and it involves two categories of action—virtues and vices. To determine the moral vision of a given story, we can simply list the virtues the story offers for approval and the vices it wants us to reject. The chief embodiments of virtues and vices in a story are the characters, who are, after all, moral examples. While making such a list can lead to reading stories simplistically and moralizing, it does not need to do so, and in any case, this is simply how stories embody morality. The alternative would be for storytellers to preach, and that is not how great literature secures its effects.

The virtues that we observe as we proceed through *The Lion, the Witch and the Wardrobe* are chiefly the following: loyalty, honesty, hospitality, generosity, courage, self-sacrifice and selflessness more generally. The vices are chiefly these: betrayal, deceitfulness, tyranny, cruelty, greed and selfishness.

Writers who espouse a moral vision in their stories root that morality in certain underlying principles. For example, a moral vision presupposes the existence of good and evil and a way of differentiating between them. A related premise is that people have the ability to make moral choices and are not coerced to behave as they do. Further, a moral vision implies a view of the person—assuming, for example, that people are both good and bad, that the choices they make are momentous and that they are responsible for their actions.

ℭ *For Reflection or Discussion*

- Compile your list of virtues and vices for *The Lion, the Witch and the Wardrobe*.
- How does the author get you to approve and disapprove of these?
- These virtues and vices are embodied in the characters and their actions. Try linking each of the vices and virtues, then, with specific characters and events in the story.
- Now that you have codified your understanding of the moral vision of the book, how Christian do you think that moral vision is? Would you label it inclusively Christian or exclusively Christian?

THEOLOGICAL THEMES IN *THE LION, THE WITCH AND THE WARDROBE*

A final aspect of the Christian vision of *The Lion, the Witch and the Wardrobe* is the religious ideas that it embodies and espouses. The most important theological fact about this novel is its christological focus. The figure of Aslan dominates our experience of the book, and Aslan is representative of Christ. The redemptive acts of Aslan, coupled with his coming back to life after an atoning death, symbolically render the story of Christ's passion and resurrection. This story of salvation history is told with theological precision and with a continuous eye to the Gospel accounts of the life and death of Jesus.

A second overarching theological reality of the book is a great spiritual conflict between good and evil. The Bible forms a subtext for this thread in the story, too, because the story of cosmic conflict organizes the Bible from start to finish. Lewis himself provides one of the best ways of formulating this aspect of the Christian worldview. In a printed debate on the subject of recreation, Lewis claimed that in a Christian view of the world "there is no neutral ground in the universe: every square inch, every split second, is claimed by God and counterclaimed by Satan." For *The Lion, the Witch and the Wardrobe*, we can substitute the names Aslan and the White Witch.

The Lion, the Witch and the Wardrobe asserts the power of evil in the universe. We can trace this story of evil on multiple levels. In its most terrifying reaches, evil is given a supernatural identity. Only slightly less fearsome is the evil that the forces of nature can inflict on people. But the examples of evil that are most pervasive are also the most familiar to us: the evil that people do, both to themselves and to others. It is obvious that Lewis borrowed a page from Shakespeare and Milton in his portrayal of the self-destructiveness of evil and its ability to infect a whole society.

The possibility of goodness in the universe, in human society and in individuals is also a leading theme of *The Lion, the Witch and the Wardrobe*. We see the good on multiple levels. We see it preeminently in Aslan, of course, but also in nature. And the story gives us memorable pictures of good persons in their best moments.

The book also provides glimpses of the eschaton—the final end with its accompanying destruction of evil and the triumph of the good. The world of Narnia itself poses something of a mystery or ambiguity here. In many ways, Narnia is an analogue to life on earth. We look at metaphors of the human condition as we travel with the children through Narnia. But at other points in *The Lion, the Witch and the Wardrobe,* and especially in the last two chapters, we intuitively assimilate the action in the spirit with which we read the biblical book of Revelation, with its pictures of the final end. The turning of the statues back into people, a gigantic and decisive last battle, coronations at a great hall, living "in great joy" and remembering "life in this world . . . only as one remembers a dream"—all of these have an eschatological feel to them.

For Reflection or Discussion

Lewis praised Edmund Spenser's *Faerie Queene* for its way of inviting both a child's response and a sophisticated and intellectual adult response. Part of the genius of the Narnian stories is their ability to elicit the same double response.

- Even though we do not hear anything definite about Aslan until nearly halfway through the book, and although he enters the story as an active character considerably later than that, the characterization of Aslan is the single most important facet of this story. Focus on the parts of the story that describe Aslan and reflect on this description as a portrait of the person and work of Christ.
- The Bible forms a continuous frame of reference and literary model for *The Lion, the Witch and the Wardrobe.* What are the ways in which the story draws on the Bible as an assumed frame of reference?
- The Christian doctrines listed above are only a beginning. What other religious themes strike you as being important in the book?

22

A Brief Biography of C. S. Lewis

Clive Staples Lewis was born on November 29, 1898, in Belfast, northern Ireland. His father, Albert, was a lawyer in the Belfast Police Courts, and his mother, Flora, was the daughter of a prominent Church of Ireland clergyman. Young Clive's early years were spent in a happy and secure home. His only sibling was a brother, Warren, who was three years his senior. The two boys were close friends from an early age and indeed remained so throughout their lives. As children, they shared a variety of interests and spent many happy hours together in activities such as riding bicycles, playing on the beach, drawing, writing stories and reading books.

As a young child, Clive rechristened himself with the nickname Jacksie (later shortened to Jack), and it was by this designation that he was henceforth known to his family and close friends. When Jack was only nine years old, his much-loved mother fell ill and died from cancer. Understandably, this was one of the most painful events of his life. Shortly after this, he was sent off to boarding school in England with his brother Warren. This separation from home at such a difficult time contributed to a gulf that was gradually widening between Albert and his sons. Unfortunately, the estrangement was compounded by the fact that the boarding school itself was a very poor one, run by an emotionally unstable headmaster. With cause, Jack and Warren were both miserable during their years as students there.

Eventually, after several subsequent schools, Jack ended up studying under a private tutor, W. T. Kirkpatrick, in Great Bookham, Surrey. His years with Kirkpatrick were not only extremely idyllic ones but also academically rewarding, as the teenage Jack benefited greatly from the rigorous educational methods of this brilliant teacher. As a result of Kirkpatrick's excellent instruction, in December 1916 Jack earned a scholarship to University College, Oxford.

A short time after Jack entered the university, however, his studies were interrupted when he was called to active service in the trenches of World War I France. After being wounded at the Battle of Arras in 1918, he was given a medical discharge from the army. He returned to Oxford, where he performed with excellence, receiving three First Class degrees. In 1924 he was elected to a Fellowship in English Language and Literature at Magdalen College, Oxford, where he remained for almost thirty years. In 1954, toward the end of his teaching years, he accepted a professorship at Magdalene College, Cambridge. Lewis's academic career was a distinguished one, resulting in the publication of numerous scholarly texts, including *The Allegory of Love* (1936), *A Preface to "Paradise Lost"* (1942), *English Literature in the Sixteenth Century, excluding Drama* (1954) and *An Experiment in Criticism* (1961).

Though raised in a Christian home, Lewis had become an atheist during his schooldays in England. The complete story of his return to the Christian faith as an adult convert is recorded in his autobiography, *Surprised by Joy* (1955). In this account he describes his experiences with *joy,* the term he gave to his periodic feelings of inconsolable longing. He came to realize that these experiences of unsatisfied desire were actually divine intimations pointing to a transcendent reality beyond our material world. In addition, his encounters with works by authors such as George MacDonald and G. K. Chesterton and his discussions with Christian friends such as J. R. R. Tolkien helped him to overcome his intellectual and emotional barriers to faith. Lewis returned to a belief in Christianity in 1931.

After becoming a Christian, Lewis quickly attempted to use his gifts as a writer to communicate his faith. These publications remain among his most far-reaching and influential works. Indeed, Lewis's singular ability to use imaginative language to depict and clarify theological truths, coupled with his intentional avoidance of sectarian issues and his accomplished skill at rational argument, enabled him to be a powerful voice for the central realities of the Christian faith. The best known of his apologetic volumes is *Mere Christianity*. Among his works of fiction, his seven Chronicles of Narnia are classics in the field of children's literature and demonstrate the distinctive capacity of fantasy to embody spiritual truths. Through both his religious prose and his fiction, Lewis not only spoke compellingly to unbelievers but also nurtured the faith of fellow Christians.

A longtime bachelor, Lewis was married late in life to an American writer, Joy Davidman, a union that brought him great happiness. Sadly, their married life together was very brief, as Joy died from cancer after just three short years together. Lewis was grief-stricken by his loss, and he survived his wife by only a few years, dying on November 22, 1963. Decades after his death, C. S. Lewis continues to be one of the most widely read authors of our time.

KEY DATES IN THE LIFE OF C. S. LEWIS

1898	Born in Belfast, northern Ireland (November 29)
1908	Death of his mother
1914	Goes to study with private tutor Kirkpatrick
1917	Begins studies at Oxford University
1917	On the frontlines of World War I France
1919	Returns to his studies at Oxford
1925	Elected a Fellow of Magdalen College, Oxford
1929	Becomes a theist
1929	Death of his father
1931	Returns to a belief in Christianity
1933	Publishes his first book discussing the Christian faith (*The Pilgrim's Regress*)
1942	Publication of *The Screwtape Letters*

1950   Receives his first letter from Joy Davidman Gresham

1950   Publication of *The Lion, the Witch and the Wardrobe*

1951   Publication of *Prince Caspian*

1952   Publication of *Mere Christianity*

1952   Publication of *The Voyage of the "Dawn Treader"*

1953   Publication of *The Silver Chair*

1954   Publication of *The Horse and His Boy*

1955   Publication of *The Magician's Nephew*

1955   Publication of his autobiography, *Surprised by Joy*

1956   Marries Joy Davidman Gresham in civil ceremony (April 23)

1956   Joy is diagnosed with cancer (October)

1956   Publication of the seventh and final volume of the Chronicles of Narnia *(The Last Battle)*

1957   Marries Joy in Anglican ceremony at her hospital bedside (March 21)

1960   Death of Joy Davidman Lewis (July 13)

1960   Publication of *The Four Loves*

1961   Publication of *A Grief Observed*

1963   Death of C. S. Lewis (November 22)

Appendix
What Is the Correct Order
in Which to Read the Chronicles of Narnia?

Should one read the seven Narnian books in the order in which they were published or according to the chronology of the history of Narnia? This question has become a subject of debate among both general readers and Lewis scholars. Here is the order of original publication:

- *The Lion, the Witch and the Wardrobe* (1950)
- *Prince Caspian* (1951)
- *The Voyage of the "Dawn Treader"* (1952)
- *The Silver Chair* (1953)
- *The Horse and His Boy* (1954)
- *The Magician's Nephew* (1955)
- *The Last Battle* (1956)

Here is the order in which the history of Narnia unfolds (the "chronological order"):

- *The Magician's Nephew*
- *The Lion, the Witch and the Wardrobe*
- *The Horse and His Boy*
- *Prince Caspian*
- *The Voyage of the "Dawn Treader"*
- *The Silver Chair*
- *The Last Battle*

Those who choose the chronological order of Narnian history base their decision on C. S. Lewis's own statements—first in a letter of April 23, 1957, to a young boy, and some years later when Lewis reaffirmed this preference in a conversation with Walter Hooper. However, in spite of these comments by Lewis, there are many who believe that the publication order is to be preferred, and we are among them. The reasons for this are quite simple.

First of all, Lewis as literary critic (which is the formula we are using for this guide) makes it clear that the author does not always know best about the meaning of his own story: "It is the author who *intends;* the book *means.* . . . Of a book's meaning, in this sense, its author is not necessarily the best, and is never a perfect, judge." Elsewhere Lewis writes, "An author doesn't necessarily understand the meaning of his own story better than anyone else." As these statements illustrate, as *literary critic* Lewis was well aware of an author's own limitations in assessing not his intention but the imaginative impact or meaning that results from his work. While not ignoring Lewis's comments, then, we still need to look to the works themselves to tell us which is truly the preferred reading order.

This brings us to a second consideration: Lewis did not anticipate the other six Narnian stories when he wrote his first volume. As a result, he created this story as a "stand-alone" narrative, and the development of this first tale was not written to take into account any subsequent books. Why is this important? When Lewis was composing *The Lion, the Witch and the Wardrobe,* he intentionally used literary devices such as foreshadowing to build up reader interest and suspense. As a gifted writer, Lewis used these devices often and effectively. The excitement, the uncertainty, the unknown are all part of the wonderful experience that comes to us as the story unfolds.

To read *The Magician's Nephew* first would be to undercut the very fabric by which Lewis so carefully constructed his previous tale. Once readers know "all about" Narnia, they can no longer experience the full strangeness of Lucy's discovery of a mysterious world within the wardrobe. They do not wonder with her about the odd crunching underfoot, the unexplained dampness of the snow and the inexplicable prickly pine branches she encounters as she enters what she thought was a common, everyday wardrobe.

If the reader first experiences Narnia by reading *The Magician's Nephew,* all of this significant suspense is lost.

The most critical way that having this foreknowledge would defeat what Lewis intends can be seen in the book's deliberate and gradual introduction to the figure of Aslan. So methodical is Lewis in this unfolding revelation that the reader does not even hear about Aslan until all the way into chapter 7, when Mr. Beaver tells the children, "Aslan is on the move." To make certain that the importance of this announcement is not lost on the children, Lewis, as narrator, goes on to explain,

> And now a very curious thing happened. *None of the children knew who Aslan was any more than you do;* but the moment the Beaver had spoken these words everyone felt quite different. Perhaps it has sometimes happened to you in a dream that someone says something which you don't understand but in the dream it feels as if it had some enormous meaning—either a terrifying one which turns the whole dream into a nightmare or else a lovely meaning too lovely to put into words, which makes the dream so beautiful that you remember it all your life and are always wishing you could get into that dream again. It was like that now. At the name of Aslan each one of the children felt something jump in its inside. (*LWW,* ch. 7, pp. 67-68, emphasis ours)

Readers who have begun the series with *The Magician's Nephew* unintentionally forfeit the opportunity to experience this stirring revelation as Lewis originally intended it to be received. And the true importance of this moment extends beyond simple suspenseful anticipation. Hearing the *unexplained* phrase "Aslan is on the move" is one of those significant occasions where the story is able to arouse an affective response within the reader, speaking imaginatively to the heart, rather than to the head.

A true-life example of this can be found in the response of three-year-old Ryan, who discovered *The Lion, the Witch and the Wardrobe* on his bedroom bookshelf and asked to have the story read to him. Finding it easier to comply than to dissuade him from his choice, and assuming that the toddler would quickly grow bored with the advanced story, his mother began to read aloud from the book. So it was that without context or discussion, the story was gradually read, chapter by chapter, to the captivated young listener. This reading pattern continued until one evening, having just heard chapter 7, Ryan sidled up to a dinner guest (fortunately a high school English teacher who knew and loved the Narnian tales) and in a whisper confided: "Have you heard? Aslan is on the move!"

What happened inside this young listener is an example of the affective response that is evoked through the storyteller's art. This response would be devastatingly weakened if the identity of Aslan was known by the reader in advance. Indeed, young Ryan's response was made on the intuitive level. He did not *know* who or what Aslan was, but he responded imaginatively to the sense of heightened anticipation Lewis had created in this powerful sequence.

This type of response is insightfully described by J. R. R. Tolkien in his essay "On Fairy-stories":

It is the mark of a good fairy-story, of the higher or more complete kind, that however wild its events, however fantastic or terrible the adventures, it can give to child or man that hears it, when the "turn" comes, a catch of the breath, a beat and lifting of the heart, near to (or indeed accompanied by) tears, as keen as that given by any form of literary art, and having a peculiar quality.

In other words, through the storyteller's art, a sense of anticipation, of deep longing for something as yet unknown, is evoked deep within the listener.

Thus we recommend that whenever possible readers begin reading the series of the seven Narnian stories with *The Lion, the Witch and the Wardrobe*.

Recommended Reading List

Duriez, Colin. *A Field Guide to Narnia*. Downers Grove, Ill.: InterVarsity Press, 2004.

Ford, Paul F. *Companion to Narnia*. Rev. ed. San Francisco: HarperSanFrancisco, 2005.

Hein, Rolland. *Christian Mythmakers*. 2nd ed. Chicago: Cornerstone Press Chicago, 2002.

Hooper, Walter. *C. S. Lewis: Companion and Guide*. San Francisco: HarperCollins, 1996.

————. *Past Watchful Dragons*. New York: Collier, 1980.

Kilby, Clyde S. *The Christian World of C. S. Lewis*. Grand Rapids, Mich.: Eerdmans, 1964.

Lewis, C. S. *An Experiment in Criticism*. Cambridge: Cambridge University Press, 1961.

————. *Letters of C. S. Lewis*. Rev. and enlarged ed. Edited by Walter Hooper. London: Collins/Fount Paperbacks, 1988.

————. *Letters to Children*. Edited by Lyle W. Dorsett and Marjorie Lamp Mead. New York: Macmillan, 1985.

————. *The Lion, the Witch and the Wardrobe*. New York: HarperCollins, 1994.

————. *On Stories and Other Essays on Literature*. New York: Harcourt Brace Jovanovich, 1982.

————. *Surprised by Joy: The Shape of My Early Life*. New York: Harcourt, Brace and World, 1955.

Martin, Thomas L., ed. *Reading the Classics with C. S. Lewis*. Grand Rapids, Mich.: Baker, 2000.

Schakel, Peter J. *Imagination and the Arts in C. S. Lewis*. Columbia: University of Missouri Press, 2002.

————. *The Way into Narnia: A Reader's Guide*. Grand Rapids, Mich.: Eerdmans, 2005.

Schultz, Jeffrey D., and John G. West Jr., eds. *The C. S. Lewis Reader's Encyclopedia*. Grand Rapids, Mich.: Zondervan, 1998.

Tolkien, J. R. R. "On Fairy-Stories." In *The Tolkien Reader*. New York: Ballantine Books, 1966.

Biographical

Dorsett, Lyle W. *A Love Observed: Joy Davidman's Life and Marriage to C. S. Lewis*. Wheaton, Ill.: Harold Shaw Publishers, 1998. (Formerly titled *And God Came In.*)

Green, Roger Lancelyn, and Walter Hooper. *C. S. Lewis: A Biography*. Fully rev. and expanded ed. London: HarperCollins, 2002.

Gresham, Douglas. *Jack's Life*. Nashville: Broadman & Holman, 2005.

Jacobs, Alan. *The Narnian: The Life and Imagination of C. S. Lewis*. San Francisco: HarperSanFrancisco, 2005.

Sayer, George. *Jack: A Life of C. S. Lewis*. Wheaton, Ill.: Crossway Books, 1994.

Notes

Introduction

Page 10   "Oddly as it may sound": C. S. Lewis, *The Allegory of Love* (New York: Oxford University Press, 1936, 1958), p. 345.

Page 11   Recommendations for how to read Spenser's *Faerie Queene:* C. S. Lewis, *Studies in Medieval and Renaissance Literature,* ed. Walter Hooper (Cambridge: Cambridge University Press, 1966), pp. 132-33, italics added.

Page 12   "Everything began with images": C. S. Lewis, "Sometimes Fairy Stories May Say Best What's to Be Said," in *On Stories and Other Essays on Literature* (New York: Harcourt Brace Jovanovich, 1982), p. 46.

Page 12   "[Lewis] wanted the moral and spiritual significance": George Sayer, *Jack: A Life of C. S. Lewis* (Wheaton, Ill.: Crossway, 1994), p. 256.

Page 12   To look, listen, surrender and receive, as Lewis advised . . . "we shall be deliciously surprised": the advice comes from p. 19, the quote from p. 134, in C. S. Lewis, *An Experiment in Criticism* (Cambridge: Cambridge University Press, 1961).

Page 13   "I thought I saw how stories of this kind": Lewis, "Sometimes Fairy Stories May Say Best," p. 47.

Page 14   "Over twenty years ago a college English professor": Katherine Paterson, *Gates of Excellence: On Reading and Writing Books for Children* (New York: Elsevier/Nelson, 1981), p. 60.

Page 14   "A children's story which is enjoyed only by children": C. S. Lewis, "On Three Ways of Writing for Children," in *On Stories and Other Essays on Literature* (New York: Harcourt Brace Jovanovich, 1982), p. 33. His declaration that he likes fairy tales better as an adult is from pp. 34-35.

Page 15   "Let us be quite clear": Lewis, *Experiment in Criticism,* p. 38, italics added.

Page 15   "Re-reading old favourites": C. S. Lewis's letter of February 1932 in
               They Stand Together: The Letters of C. S. Lewis to Arthur Greeves (1914-
               1963), ed. Walter Hooper (London: Collins, 1979), p. 439.

Chapter 1: Lucy Looks into a Wardrobe

Page 19   "The first welling of life": Donald Newlove, *First Paragraphs: Inspired*
               Openings for Writers and Readers (New York: St. Martin's, 1992), p. 2.

Page 19   "Every novelist" box: Georgianne Ensign, *Great Beginnings: Opening*
               Lines of Great Novels (New York: HarperCollins, 1993), p. 2.

Page 21   "There is a clear sense": C. S. Lewis, *An Experiment in Criticism* (Cam-
               bridge: Cambridge University Press, 1961), p. 68.

Page 21   "The best opening for a story": Thomas Howard, "Myth: Flight to Re-
               ality," in *The Christian Imagination: The Practice of Faith in Literature and*
               Writing, ed. Leland Ryken (Colorado Springs, Colo.: Harold Shaw,
               2002), p. 339.

Page 22   Lewis's stories "were not told to actual children" ("C. S. Lewis and
               Children" box): Roger Lancelyn Green, *C. S. Lewis* (New York:
               Henry Z. Walck, 1963), p. 55.

Page 22   "I theoretically hold" ("C. S. Lewis and Children" box): C. S. Lewis,
               They Stand Together: The Letters of C. S. Lewis to Arthur Greeves (1914-
               1963), ed. Walter Hooper (London: Collins, 1979), p. 476.

Page 22   "No, I didn't start" ("C. S. Lewis and Children" box): C. S. Lewis, *Let-*
               ters to Children, ed. Lyle W. Dorsett and Marjorie Lamp Mead (New
               York: Macmillan, 1985) p. 51.

Page 25   "I am a product" ("Little Lea" box): C. S. Lewis, *Surprised by Joy: The*
               Shape of My Early Life (New York: Harcourt, Brace and World, 1955),
               p. 10.

Page 25   "Disdaining to be tied": Philip Sidney, *An Apology for Poetry,* in *Criti-*
               cism: The Major Statements, ed. Charles Kaplan (New York: St. Martin's,
               1975), p. 113.

Page 25   "To limitless freedom": C. S. Lewis, *English Literature in the Sixteenth Cen-*
               tury excluding Drama (Oxford: Oxford University Press, 1954), p. 322.

Page 26   Reminiscences of Lewis's cousin ("Lewis Family Wardrobe" box): Let-
               ter from Claire Clapperton to Clyde S. Kilby, August 20, 1979.

Page 27   "The *Lion* all began" (box): C. S. Lewis, "It All Began with a Picture,"
               in *On Stories and Other Essays on Literature* (New York: Harcourt Brace
               Jovanovich, 1982), p. 53.

Page 27   "Jocundity and jollity": C. S. Lewis, *Spenser's Images of Life,* ed. Alastair
              Fowler (Cambridge: Cambridge University Press, 1967), p. 83).

Chapter 2: What Lucy Found There

Page 30   C. S. Lewis's explorations of the utopia genre are in his *English Litera-
              ture in the Sixteenth Century excluding Drama* (Oxford: Oxford Univer-
              sity Press, 1954), pp. 167-70. "A thread of serious thought" is from
              that work, p. 170.

Page 31   Thomas More "says many things for the fun of them" ("Imaginary
              World of Boxen" box): ibid.

Page 32   "He does not keep our noses": ibid.

Page 32   Lewis's "Britishness": Philip Graham Ryken, "C. S. Lewis as the Patron
              Saint of American Evangelicalism," *Canadian C. S. Lewis Journal,*
              Spring 1998, p. 15.

Chapter 3: Edmund and the Wardrobe

Page 36   "Characters about whose fates we are made to care": Sheldon Sacks,
              Fiction and the Shape of Belief (Berkeley: University of California Press,
              1964), pp. 15, 25.

Page 36   "In most good stories" (box): Flannery O'Connor, *Mystery and Man-
              ners,* ed. Sally Fitzgerald and Robert Fitzgerald (New York: Farrar,
              Straus and Giroux, 1957), pp. 105-6.

Page 37   "Any character in a serious novel": ibid., p. 167.

Page 37   "Describe so well a certain spiritual region": C. S. Lewis, *Selected Liter-
              ary Essays,* ed. Walter Hooper (Cambridge: Cambridge University
              Press, 1969), p. 101.

Page 39   "The principle of art" (box): C. S. Lewis, *Reflections on the Psalms* (New
              York: Harcourt, Brace and World, 1958), p. 4.

Chapter 4: Turkish Delight

Page 41   "Any of the immemorial patterns": Leslie Fiedler, "Archetype and Sig-
              nature" in *Myths and Motifs in Literature,* ed. David J. Burrows et al.
              (New York: Free Press, 1973), p. 28.

Page 42   "Answering the question" (box): Peter J. Schakel, *Reading with the
              Heart: The Way into Narnia* (Grand Rapids, Mich.: Eerdmans, 1979),
              pp. 6-7. Schakel's book is a thoroughgoing application of archetypal
              criticism to the Narnian books.

Page 42   Lewis's discussion of stock themes, archetypes, "giants, dragons, . . .
                 and the like": C. S. Lewis, *A Preface to "Paradise Lost"* (New York: Ox-
                 ford University Press, 1942), pp. 48, 52, 57-59.

Page 42   "Spenser's symbols embody": C. S. Lewis, *Studies in Medieval and Re-
                 naissance Literature,* ed. Walter Hooper (Cambridge: Cambridge Uni-
                 versity Press, 1966), p. 143.

Page 42   Lewis's archetypal criticism is found in C. S. Lewis, *Spenser's Images of
                 Life,* ed. Alastair Fowler (Cambridge: Cambridge University Press,
                 1967).

Page 43   "All themes and characters" ("For Reflection or Discussion" box):
                 Northrop Frye, *The Educated Imagination* (Bloomington, Ind.: Indiana
                 University Press, 1964), pp. 48-49.

Page 43   "The Bible itself is a book of archetypes": see Leland Ryken, James C.
                 Wilhoit and Tremper Longman III, eds., *Dictionary of Biblical Imagery*
                 (Downers Grove, Ill.: InterVarsity Press, 1998).

Page 44   "The Witch is of course Circe": C. S. Lewis, letter to Prof. William L.
                 Kinter, July 30, 1954, in Schakel, *Reading with the Heart,* p. 9 (original
                 letter in the Bodleian Library, Oxford University; copy at the Wade
                 Center).

Chapter 5: Back on This Side of the Door

Page 49   An autobiographical allegory ("Reality, Reason and Faith" box): C. S.
                 Lewis, *The Pilgrim's Regress* (London: Geoffrey Bles, 1943).

Page 49   "Realism of presentation" and "realism of content": C. S. Lewis, *An Ex-
                 periment in Criticism* (Cambridge: Cambridge University Press, 1961),
                 pp. 57-59.

Page 49   "We all know that Art": Pablo Picasso, "Picasso Speaks," *Arts* 3 (1923):
                 315.

Page 50   "The word 'lifelike'" (box): C. S. Lewis, *Studies in Medieval and Renais-
                 sance Literature,* ed. Walter Hooper (Cambridge: Cambridge Univer-
                 sity Press, 1966), p. 135.

Page 50   Details in fictional stories are "not . . . mistaken for realities": Samuel
                 Johnson, "Preface to Shakespeare," in *Criticism: The Major Statements,*
                 ed. Charles Kaplan (New York: St. Martin's, 1965), p. 264.

Page 52   "We have to take reality" (box): C. S. Lewis, *Mere Christianity* (New
                 York: Macmillan, 1958), p. 48.

Chapter 6: Into the Forest

Page 53   *"The Three Musketeers* makes no appeal"* (box): C. S. Lewis, "On Stories," in *On Stories and Other Essays on Literature* (New York: Harcourt Brace Jovanovich, 1982), pp. 7, 11.

Page 54   "It is from the kind of world": Flannery O'Connor, *Mystery and Manners,* ed. Sally Fitzgerald and Robert Fitzgerald (New York: Farrar, Straus and Giroux, 1957), p. 75, italics added.

Page 54   "All writers . . . must have": Joyce Cary, *Art and Reality: Ways of the Creative Process* (Garden City, N.Y.: Doubleday, 1961), p. 174.

Page 54   "An inhabitant of its world": C. S. Lewis, *Spenser's Images of Life,* ed. Alastair Fowler (Cambridge: Cambridge University Press, 1967), p. 140.

Page 54   "Quests and wanderings": C. S. Lewis, *Studies in Medieval and Renaissance Literature,* ed. Walter Hooper (Cambridge: Cambridge University Press, 1966), p. 126.

Page 54   "The happiness which [*The Wind in the Willows*] presents": Lewis, "On Stories," p. 14.

Page 55   The fairy stories "that do not just tell us" (box): Frederick Buechner, *Telling the Truth: The Gospel as Tragedy, Comedy and Fairy Tale* (San Francisco: Harper & Row, 1977), pp. 76-78.

Page 56   Narnian time's intersection with English time ("Entering Narnia" box): Roger Lancelyn Green and Walter Hooper, *C. S. Lewis: A Biography,* rev. and exp. ed. (London: HarperCollins, 2002).

Page 56   "In the Perilous Realm": J. R. R. Tolkien, "On Fairy-Stories," in *The Tolkien Reader* (New York: Ballantine, 1966), p. 9.

Chapter 7: A Day with the Beavers

Page 58   The good place motif in the Bible: see "The Good Life," in *Dictionary of Biblical Imagery,* ed. Leland Ryken, James C. Wilhoit and Tremper Longman III (Downers Grove, Ill.: InterVarsity Press, 1998), pp. 342-43.

Page 58   Lewis notes "the presence" (box): C. S. Lewis, "On Three Ways of Writing for Children," in *On Stories and Other Essays on Literature* (New York: Harcourt Brace Jovanovich, 1982), p. 36.

Page 59   "Sometimes, as in the happy endings" (box): Northrop Frye, *The Educated Imagination* (Bloomington, Ind.: Indiana University Press, 1964), pp. 97-98.

Page 59   "Once upon a time, a very very very *long* time ago": from Scott Rice,
              ed., *It Was a Dark and Stormy Night* (New York: Penguin, 1984), p. 53.

Chapter 8: What Happened After Dinner

Page 60   "Writing about John Milton's Satan": C. S. Lewis, *A Preface to "Paradise
              Lost"* (New York: Oxford University Press, 1942), pp. 100-101.

Page 61   The final effect of a story "depended heavily": Sheldon Sacks, *Fiction
              and the Shape of Belief* (Berkeley: University of California Press, 1964),
              p. 249.

Page 61   "Goodness is bereft of its proper beauty": J. R. R. Tolkien, "On Fairy-
              Stories," in *The Tolkien Reader* (New York: Ballantine, 1966), p. 65.

Page 62   "In the fairy tales, side by side": C. S. Lewis, "On Three Ways of Writ-
              ing for Children," in *On Stories and Other Essays on Literature* (New
              York: Harcourt Brace Jovanovich, 1982), p. 32.

Page 63   "By an allegory I mean": C. S. Lewis, *Letters of C. S. Lewis,* ed. Walter
              Hooper, rev. and enl. ed. (London: Collins/Fount, 1988), p. 475.

Page 63   "An invention giving an imaginary answer": ibid., pp. 475-76.

Page 63   "Some people seem to think": C. S. Lewis, "Sometimes Fairy Stories
              May Say Best What's to Be Said," in *On Stories and Other Essays on Lit-
              erature* (New York: Harcourt Brace Jovanovich, 1982), p. 46.

Page 64   "You are mistaken when you think": C. S. Lewis, *Letters to Children,* ed.
              Lyle W. Dorsett and Marjorie Lamp Mead (New York: Macmillan,
              1985) pp. 44-45.

Page 65   "My own love": Philip Graham Ryken, "C. S. Lewis as the Patron Saint
              of American Evangelicalism," *Canadian C. S. Lewis Journal,* Spring
              1998, p. 19.

Page 65   One "can't *really* love Aslan more" (box): Lewis, *Letters to Children,* pp.
              52-53.

Page 66   "I found the name in the notes" (box): ibid., p. 29.

Chapter 9: In the Witch's House

Page 68   "Among stories whose artistic authenticity" (box): Simon O. Lesser,
              Fiction and the Unconscious (Chicago: University of Chicago Press,
              1975), pp. 54-55.

Page 69   "I often saw [C. S. Lewis] from the windows": Barbara Reynolds,
              "Memories of C. S. Lewis in Cambridge," *Chesterton Review* 17, nos. 3-
              4: 380.

Chapter 10: The Spell Begins to Break

Page 72   "A hard poet [to understand]": C. S. Lewis, *Studies in Medieval and Renaissance Literature,* ed. Walter Hooper (Cambridge: Cambridge University Press, 1966), p. 132.

Page 75   Father Christmas "does not seem to fit quite comfortably": Roger Lancelyn Green and Walter Hooper, *C. S. Lewis: A Biography,* rev. and exp. ed. (London: HarperCollins, 2002), p. 307.

Chapter 11: Aslan Is Nearer

Page 76   "No critics seem to me farther astray" (box): C. S. Lewis, *English Literature in the Sixteenth Century excluding Drama* (Oxford: Oxford University Press, 1954), p. 389.

Page 78   "And treat it in such a way" (about the *Aeneid*): C. S. Lewis, *A Preface to "Paradise Lost"* (New York: Oxford University Press, 1942), p. 34.

Page 80   Milton's "unremitting *manipulation*": ibid., p. 41.

Page 81   Shakespeare's skill "of course . . . affects those": Lewis, *English Literature in the Sixteenth Century,* p. 508.

Page 81   "To some, I am afraid" (box): ibid.

Chapter 12: Peter's First Battle

Page 86   "To confuse children and add to their fears": Madeleine L'Engle, "Is It Good Enough for Children?" in *The Christian Imagination: The Practice of Faith in Literature and Writing,* ed. Leland Ryken (Colorado Springs, Colo.: Harold Shaw, 2002), p. 428.

Page 86   "Haunting, disabling": C. S. Lewis, "On Three Ways of Writing for Children," in *On Stories and Other Essays on Literature* (New York: Harcourt Brace Jovanovich, 1982), p. 39.

Page 87   "The knowledge that he is born" (box): ibid., pp. 39-40.

Chapter 13: Deep Magic from the Dawn of Time

Page 88   "Metaphors of the human condition": Ursula K. Le Guin, *The Language of the Night: Essays on Fantasy and Science Fiction* (New York: G. P. Putnam's Sons, 1979), p. 58.

Page 88   "We who hobnob with hobbits" (box): ibid., pp. 57-58.

Chapter 14: The Triumph of the Witch

Page 94   "A work of (whatever) art" C. S. Lewis, *An Experiment in Criticism*

(Cambridge: Cambridge University Press, 1961), p. 88, italics added.

Page 97   "At first there wasn't . . . that element pushed itself in": C. S. Lewis, "Sometimes Fairy Stories May Say Best What's to Be Said," in *On Stories and Other Essays on Literature* (New York: Harcourt Brace Jovanovich, 1982), p. 46.

Page 97   Literature "rescues the most admitted truths" ("Past Watchful Dragons" box): Samuel Taylor Coleridge, *Biographia Literaria* in *The Norton Anthology of English Literature,* 7th ed. (New York: W. W. Norton, 2001), p. 1626.

Page 97   "I thought I saw" ("Past Watchful Dragons" box): Lewis, "Sometimes Fairy Stories May Say Best," p. 47.

Page 98   "The only moral that is of any value": C. S. Lewis, "On Three Ways of Writing for Children," in *On Stories and Other Essays on Literature* (New York: Harcourt Brace Jovanovich, 1982), p. 42.

Chapter 15: Deeper Magic from Before the Dawn of Time

Page 100   "Joy, Joy beyond the walls": J. R. R. Tolkien, "On Fairy-Stories," in *The Tolkien Reader* (New York: Ballantine, 1966), p. 68.

Page 100   "It is the mark of a good fairy-story" (box): ibid., pp. 68-69.

Page 101   "There has never been an age" (text and box): Frederick Buechner, *Telling the Truth: The Gospel as Tragedy, Comedy and Fairy Tale* (San Francisco: Harper & Row, 1977), pp. 75-76.

Page 102   "Beasts talk and flowers come alive": ibid., p. 79.

Page 102   Fairy stories "arouse, and imaginatively satisfy": C. S. Lewis, "On Three Ways of Writing for Children," in *On Stories and Other Essays on Literature* (New York: Harcourt Brace Jovanovich, 1982), pp. 37-38.

Page 102   "Fairy-stories were plainly not primarily concerned": Tolkien, "On Fairy-Stories," pp. 40, 46.

Page 102   "Beneath the specific events": Buechner, *Telling the Truth,* p. 81.

Page 103   "It is of course much more": C. S. Lewis, *Studies in Medieval and Renaissance Literature,* ed. Walter Hooper (Cambridge: Cambridge University Press, 1966), p. 133.

Page 103   The *Faerie Queen*'s "primary appeal" (box): ibid., pp. 132-33.

Page 103   Lewis "wrote fairy tales because" ("For Reflection and Discussion" box): C. S. Lewis, "Sometimes Fairy Stories May Say Best What's to Be Said," in *On Stories and Other Essays on Literature* (New York: Harcourt Brace Jovanovich, 1982), p. 47.

Page 104   Fairy stories "seem to have certain features": Buechner, *Telling the Truth,* p. 76.

Chapter 16: What Happened About the Statues

Page 106   "Instantly . . . uplifted" ("Norse Mythology" box): C. S. Lewis, *Surprised by Joy: The Shape of My Early Life* (New York: Harcourt, Brace and World, 1955), p. 17.

Page 107   Traits of myth ("Myth" box): C. S. Lewis, *An Experiment in Criticism* (Cambridge: Cambridge University Press, 1961), pp. 43-44.

Page 108   "The resemblance between these myths": C. S. Lewis, *Reflections on the Psalms* (New York: Harcourt, Brace and World, 1958), p. 107.

Chapter 17: The Hunting of the White Stag

Page 111   "The Consolation of the Happy Ending" through "the walls of the world": J. R. R. Tolkien, "On Fairy-Stories," in *The Tolkien Reader* (New York: Ballantine, 1966), p. 68.

Page 111   "The Christian Story . . . embraces": ibid., p. 71.

Page 111   "Good and evil meet": Frederick Buechner, *Telling the Truth: The Gospel as Tragedy, Comedy and Fairy Tale* (San Francisco: Harper & Row, 1977), p. 82.

Page 112   "The Gospels contain" (box): ibid., pp. 71-73.

Page 112   "The final victory": ibid., p. 90.

Chapter 18: Retrospective

Page 117   "In our direct experience of fiction" (box): Northrop Frye, *Fables of Identity: Studies in Poetic Mythology* (New York: Harcourt, 1963), p. 22.

Page 117   "A story must be striking": Thomas Hardy, notebook entry, reprinted in *Novelists on the Novel,* ed. Miriam Allot (London: Routledge and Kegan Paul, 1959), p. 58.

Page 118   "The deep significance of life": Charles Baudelaire, quoted in J. Middleton Murry, *The Problem of Style* (London: Oxford University Press, 1922), p. 30.

Page 118   "[A masterpiece] modifies": Sheldon Sacks, *Fiction and the Shape of Belief* (Berkeley: University of California Press, 1964), p. 253.

Page 118   "We speak of a book as a classic": Harry Levin, introduction to *The Scarlet Letter and Other Tales of the Puritans* (Boston: Houghton Mifflin, 1960), p. vii.

Page 118   "[A great book] lays its images": C. S. Lewis, review of *Taliessin Through Logres, Oxford Review Magazine* 64 (March 14, 1946): 248-50.

Page 119   "What we tend to require": Nina Baym, *The Scarlet Letter: A Reading* (Boston: G. K. Hall, 1986), p. xviii.

Page 119   "Fun for the whole family": Philip Graham Ryken, "C. S. Lewis as the Patron Saint of American Evangelicalism," *Canadian C. S. Lewis Journal,* Spring 1988, p. 19.

Page 119   "It seldom loses": C. S. Lewis, *English Literature in the Sixteenth Century excluding Drama* (Oxford: Oxford University Press, 1954), p. 393.

Page 119   "The sure mark": C. S. Lewis, *An Experiment in Criticism* (Cambridge: Cambridge University Press, 1961), p. 2.

Page 119   "There is hope for a man": C. S. Lewis, "On Stories," in *On Stories and Other Essays on Literature* (New York: Harcourt Brace Jovanovich, 1982), p. 16.

Page 119   "If you find that the reader": ibid.

Page 120   "Those who read great works": Lewis, *Experiment in Criticism,* p. 2.

Page 120   "I think my growth": C. S. Lewis, "On Three Ways of Writing for Children," in *On Stories and Other Essays on Literature* (New York: Harcourt Brace Jovanovich, 1982), p. 35.

Page 120   The case of a student: Peter J. Schakel, *Imagination and the Arts in C. S. Lewis* (Columbia: University of Missouri Press, 2002), pp. 34-35.

Page 121   Suspense, surprise and curiosity about outcome live on: C. S. Lewis, "On Stories," in *On Stories and Other Essays on Literature* (New York: Harcourt Brace Jovanovich, 1982), pp. 16-17).

Chapter 19: How the Narnian Books Came to Be

Page 131   "I am not quite sure": C. S. Lewis, "On Three Ways of Writing for Children," in *On Stories and Other Essays on Literature* (New York: Harcourt Brace Jovanovich, 1982), p. 37.

Page 131   "At first I had very little idea": C. S. Lewis, "It All Began with a Picture," in *On Stories and Other Essays on Literature* (New York: Harcourt Brace Jovanovich, 1982), p. 53.

Page 132   "In a certain sense, I have never exactly": Lewis, "On Three Ways of Writing," p. 41.

Page 132   "About forty": Lewis, "It All Began," p. 53.

Page 133   At least one ill-fated children's story: C. S. Lewis, letter to Mr. and Mrs. E. L. Baxter, in *C. S. Lewis Collected Letters,* ed. Walter Hooper, vol. 2,

Books, Broadcasts and War, 1931-1949 (London: HarperCollins, 2004), p. 802.

Page 133   Lewis spoke "vaguely of completing a children's book": Chad Walsh, *C. S. Lewis: Apostle to the Skeptics* (New York: Macmillan, 1949), p. 10.

Page 133   "This [comment by Walsh] referred": Roger Lancelyn Green, *C. S. Lewis* (New York: Henry Z. Walck, 1963), pp. 36-37.

Page 133   "The Wood That Time Forgot" . . . is set in an Oxfordshire wood: Roger Lancelyn Green and Walter Hooper, *C. S. Lewis: A Biography,* rev. and exp. ed. (London: HarperCollins, 2002), p. 305.

Page 134   Not only a myth-maker but also a "myth-user": Green, *C. S. Lewis,* p. 33.

Page 134   "[A rich] background of thought": ibid., p. 34.

Page 135   The literary influence was subconscious: ibid., p. 36.

Page 136   "Ranging from the deletion of the word 'Crikey!'": Green and Hooper, *C. S. Lewis,* p. 308.

Page 137   "C. S. Lewis told me that he had actually gone": Pauline Baynes, quoted in Walter Hooper, *Past Watchful Dragons* (New York: Macmillan, 1979), p. 77.

Page 137   "The most kindly and tolerant of authors": ibid., pp. 77-78.

Page 138   "Before [that] year was out": Hooper, *Past Watchful Dragons,* pp. 30-31.

Page 138   "When I wrote the *Lion*": C. S. Lewis, *Letters of C. S. Lewis,* ed. W. H. Lewis (London: Geoffrey Bles, 1966), p. 307. The complete text of this letter to James Higgs (2 Dec. 1962) was published in *The Horn Book Magazine,* October 1966.

Page 138   Green does acknowledge: Green and Hooper, *C. S. Lewis,* p. 315.

Chapter 20: Reception History of *The Lion, the Witch and the Wardrobe*

Page 141   "[The Narnian books] are the best-known and most influential works": Peter J. Schakel, *Reading with the Heart: The Way into Narnia* (Grand Rapids, Mich.: Eerdmans, 1979), p. xi.

Page 141   "In spite of anything that can be said against them": Roger Lancelyn Green and Walter Hooper, *C. S. Lewis: A Biography,* rev. and exp. ed. (London: HarperCollins, 2002), p. 328.

Page 142   "It is an irony of literary history": Chad Walsh, *The Literary Legacy of C. S. Lewis* (New York: Harcourt Brace Jovanovich, 1979), p. 157.

Page 142   "However innocent its beginnings": John Goldthwaite, *The Natural History of Make-Believe* (New York: Oxford University Press, 1996), pp. 242-43.

Page 142   "In order to understand the meaning of such fantasies": David Hol-
            brook, *The Skeleton in the Wardrobe: C. S. Lewis's Fantasies—A Phenom-
            enological Study* (Toronto: Bucknell University Press, 1991), p. 79.

Page 143   "There is no doubt in the public mind": Philip Pullman, "The Dark
            Side of Narnia," *Guardian*, October 1, 1998, p. 6.

Page 143   "The two series resemble each other": "Philip Pullman," in *Wikipedia:
            The Free Encyclopedia*, <http://en.wikipedia.org/wiki/Philip_Pullman>.

Page 143   "Both Lewis's and Pullman's series take place": Gregg Easterbrook, "In
            Defense of C. S. Lewis," *Atlantic Monthly*, October 2001, available at
            <www.theatlantic.com/issues/2001/10/easterbrook.htm>.

Page 144   "Pullman's stories are crammed": Peter Hitchens, "A Labour of Loath-
            ing," *Spectator*, January 18, 2003, available at <www.lewrockwell.com/
            spectator/spec11.html>.

Page 144   "I was sure that I was going to write stories myself": Philip Pullman, "Philip
            Pullman: A Personal Glimpse," posted on <www.randomhouse.com/
            highschool/authors/pullman.html>.

Page 144   "To be sure, there is something to be said": Pullman, "Dark Side."

Page 145   "One may well regret": Schakel, *Reading with the Heart*, pp. 13-14.

Page 145   "I have three children, aged six to twelve": Easterbrook, "In Defense of
            C. S. Lewis."

Page 147   "Susan like Cinderella, is undergoing a transition": Pullman, "Dark
            Side." For a thoughtful response to this criticism by Pullman, see
            Mary R. Bowman, "'A Darker Ignorance': C. S. Lewis and the Nature
            of the Fall," *Mythlore*, no. 91, Summer 2003, pp. 62-78.

Page 147   "Lewis certainly had a different view of women": "Philip Pullman
            and C. S. Lewis," at Facing the Challenge of Our Times website,
            <www.facingthechallenge.org/pplewis5.htm>.

Page 148   Christians and feminists: Candice Fredrick and Sam McBride, *Women
            Among the Inklings: Gender, C. S. Lewis, J. R. R. Tolkien and Charles Wil-
            liams* (Westport, Conn.: Greenwood, 2001), p. xii.

Page 148   The flaws they perceive in Lewis do "not in any way negate": ibid., p.
            102.

Page 148   "Lewis titled this satisfying little episode": Goldthwaite, *Natural His-
            tory of Make-Believe*, pp. 241-42.

Page 149   "There is violence in the *Chronicles*": Schakel, *Reading with the Heart*,
            pp. 14-15.

Page 150   "*The Chronicles of Narnia* are one of the most powerful tools": Mary Van

Nattan, "C. S. Lewis: The Devil's Wisest Fool," ed. Steve Van Nattan, available at <www.balaams-ass.com/journal/homemake/cslewis.htm>.

Page 150   "Lewis did not share a concern": Peter J. Schakel, *Imagination and the Arts in C. S. Lewis* (Columbia: University of Missouri Press, 2002), pp. 173-74.

Page 150   "I hear you've been reading Jack's children's story": J. R. R. Tolkien, quoted in Green and Hooper, *C. S. Lewis,* p. 307.

Page 151   Tolkien's criticisms of the story were quite devastating: George Sayer, *Jack: A Life of C. S. Lewis* (Wheaton, Ill.: Crossway, 1994), pp. 312-13.

Page 151   Green originally agreed with Tolkien about the arrival of Father Christmas: Green and Hooper, *C. S. Lewis,* p. 307.

Page 151   Ruth Pitter's besting of Lewis: Ruth Pitter, "Poet to Poet," in *In Search of C. S. Lewis,* ed. Stephen Schofield (South Plainfield, N.J.: Bridge, 1983), p. 113.

Page 151   "The critical reception of the seven books was varied": Green and Hooper, *C. S. Lewis,* p. 326.

Page 152   "For children, the inner meaning": *Chosen for Children: An Account of the Books Which Have Been Awarded the Library Association Carnegie Medal, 1936-1965* (London: Library Association, 1967), p. 84.

Page 152   "The books I loved best of all": Francis Spufford, *The Child That Books Built* (New York: Henry Holt, 2002), p. 87; critical perspective on the Narnian books, p. 102.

Chapter 21: The Christian Vision of *The Lion, the Witch and the Wardrobe*

Page 156   "To judge between one *ethos* and another": C. S. Lewis, *English Literature in the Sixteenth Century excluding Drama* (Oxford: Oxford University Press, 1954), p. 331.

Page 156   "The habitual furniture of our minds": C. S. Lewis, "On Three Ways of Writing for Children," in *On Stories and Other Essays on Literature* (New York: Harcourt Brace Jovanovich, 1982), p. 42.

Page 156   "The matter . . . everything in the story": ibid.

Page 156   "Let the pictures tell you": ibid., p. 41.

Page 156   "The comments on life": C. S. Lewis, *An Experiment in Criticism* (Cambridge: Cambridge University Press, 1961), p. 84.

Page 157   "The Christian . . . has no objection": C. S. Lewis, *Christian Reflections,* ed. Walter Hooper (Grand Rapids, Mich.: Eerdmans, 1967), p. 10.

Page 157   "Christian artists do not need to be threatened": Francis A. Schaeffer,

"Perspectives on Art," in *The Christian Imagination: The Practice of Faith in Literature and Writing,* ed. Leland Ryken (Colorado Springs, Colo.: Harold Shaw, 2002), p. 46.

Page 157   "A great deal (not all) of our literature was made to be read lightly": Lewis, *Christian Reflections,* p. 34.

Page 160   "See with other eyes": Lewis, *Experiment in Criticism,* p. 137.

Page 161   "Stone, and wood, . . . tree and grass": J. R. R. Tolkien, "On Fairy-Stories," in *The Tolkien Reader* (New York: Ballantine, 1966), p. 59.

Page 162   "Strengthens our relish for real life": C. S. Lewis, "On Stories," in *On Stories and Other Essays on Literature* (New York: Harcourt Brace Jovanovich, 1982), p. 14.

Page 165   "There is no neutral ground": Lewis, *Christian Reflections,* p. 33.

Appendix

Page 171   Letter of April 23, 1957, to a young boy: C. S. Lewis, *Letters to Children,* ed. Lyle W. Dorsett and Marjorie Lamp Mead (New York: Macmillan, 1985), p. 68.

Page 172   Lewis reaffirmed this preference in a conversation with Walter Hooper: Walter Hooper, *Past Watchful Dragons* (New York: Macmillan, 1979), p. 32.

Page 172   "It is the author who *intends*": C. S. Lewis, "On Criticism," in *On Stories and Other Essays on Literature* (New York: Harcourt Brace Jovanovich, 1982), pp. 139-40.

Page 172   "An author doesn't necessarily understand": C. S. Lewis, letter to Clyde S. Kilby, February 10, 1957; see *Letters of C. S. Lewis,* ed. Walter Hooper, rev. and enl. ed. (London: Collins/Fount, 1988), p. 462.

Page 174   "It is the mark of a good fairy-story": J. R. R. Tolkien, "On Fairy-Stories," in *The Tolkien Reader* (New York: Ballantine, 1966), pp. 68-69.

Page 174   Readers interested in a fuller discussion of the issue of reading order should see Peter Schakel's excellent chapter "It Does Not Matter Very Much—or Does It? The 'Correct' Order for Reading the Chronicles," in his *Imagination and the Arts in C. S. Lewis* (Columbia: University of Missouri Press, 2002), pp. 40-52.

Acknowledgments and Permissions

Acknowledgments

We are grateful to our colleagues at the Marion E. Wade Center, Wheaton College, for the encouragement and support which they offered as we worked on this volume: Director Christopher Mitchell, Heidi Truty, Mary Dalton and Shawn Mrakovich. In addition, we are especially indebted to our graduate assistant, Jake Hanson, for his very able assistance in the checking of references, help with the preparation of the index and countless other tasks.

We would also like to thank the editorial and production staff of InterVarsity Press for their thorough and skilled work; in particular, we would like to express our appreciation to our editor, Cynthia Bunch, for her encouragement and advice throughout the editorial process.

Permissions

Index